Not Easily Broken

FA Bockari

DEDICATION

I dedicate this book to the love of my life my
daughter Gabriella, My angel I only pray that my
story will inspire you to keep fighting the battles of
life while being reassured that there will always be
a light at the end of every tunnel. God will always
be the foundation on which you stand, be brave my
love for you are my greatest blessing and every day
you are my reason to keep walking to the end of
every tunnel because I know you are my angel on
earth that was sent to hold my hand during the
times when I am afraid of the light of my own
shadow. Mummy loves today and forever more,
everything I do Gabriella I do it for you.

CONTENTS

ACKNOWLEDGMENTS

I want to take this time to thank everyone that has been a part of my journey, those that touched my life and left beautiful marks that remind me of their goodness.

To my parents, I know that you are always with me and there isn't a day that I don't yarn for your voice, smell or touch but I have accepted that you have to rest and I console myself with the joy of knowing that one day you will welcome me at the gates of heaven.

To my dearest Uncle Abu, you have always taken the role of my father in my life even before my dad passed away. You have cared for me as if I was one from my own rib and today I want you to know that I am thankful that you never turned your back on me and always did whatever it took to make sure that I was okay. You are a man of great honor and I have the highest level of love and respect for you, forever will you be my father and I pray that God's will shall always prevail in your life Uncle.

To My Uncle Francis, You are the coolest and

funniest, more than anything I enjoy how quickly your temper rises. You are a man that always wants to see the best to his family and you are always willing to stand up for those you love. Thank you Uncle for always opening your home to me, thank you for your guidance, for your endless love and support even in times when my actions may have caused you shame and pain, I love you today and forever more.

To Second Mother, My Aunty Baby:

I thank God that I found you; I thank God that I never listened to the lies because I would have missed out on the amazing mother that you have been to me. You make me laugh and never get tired of advising me about my life. You are the best grandma to Gabriella and we adore you so much because you have always shown your genuine love and support us, you have made sure that we are okay. I admire you more than you know and if I can be half of the woman that you are as a mother and wife I know that I would be okay. Thank you for carrying my burdens with me, thank you for installing hope in me, thank you for always sharing your experiences with me in order to bring positive change in my life. I am thankful and grateful for Uncle John, Bumi, Mama, Puddi, Yemisi, Junior and Musi because more than anything you are all blessed and amazing and kind hearted people and I am so proud to call you all my family. May the Lord continue to keep you all in good health and always under his wings of blessings and favour.

My dearest Koya, I am forever grateful to you for being to me what I need in my life of life and what I was lacked which was consistency. You stood by your words and never left my side no matter how dark the tunnel got, you help my hand and held through the darkness. Koya you are unique, you are kind, you are vessel of love and hope and everyone in the world needs a Koya in their life, thank you for being a part of mine and Gabriella's journey.

Tadeyo my dearest sister and friend, I remember all the times I would cry over the phone to you about whatever it was that had happened and like a true sister you never judged me or pushed me away but always asked me what you could do to make it better for me. Tadeyo I am thankful that I get to call you my friend and whenever I picture my life in every vision I see you beside me and I am grateful for you.

Mabinty I want to thank you for the grace that you showed me in my times of sorrow, thank you for being such an amazing mother figure to Gabriella throughout the years. You are such a kind hearted and selfless human being who is always there for the people you love. In my hour is need you cried with me and helped to cover my shame, only God can bless you and Tolu for all the love and kindness you have shown me and Gabriella; I love you and will forever be grateful to you my dearest sister and friend.

Samina we have come just a long way and people never understood our bond could break our bond because where two cancerians are together not can break them apart because you are twins by nature. When I think about all the pain and shame I have carried in my life you are one person that I have never been ashamed to open up too, we laugh and we cry and we've fought but my dearest sister because God is our foundation we have always overcome. You are a mirror of me and that is why I love and cherish you so much, thank you for being an amazing Aunty to Gabriella and a brilliant friend to me.

Alima I am speechless but every day I will

never stop asking God to bless you, you are true daughter of Zion with a heart as big as the ocean. You are kind and loving and funny; an amazing mother and wife and I see and respect how you love and care for those around. I am privileged to call you my friend and I am so thankful that it was in the house of God that we were connected. Thank you for standing me with in times when others walked away, I love you and every day I pray that God blesses you.

To My dearest sister Hawa, our journey hasn't always been easy but I take joy in knowing that you always have my back and are always there for me, you are kind and loving and I pray that God will always guide and protect your footsteps. Thank you for always carrying my battles as your own and forever will I stand beside you big sis.

My Diaka (BooBoo), you are a one of a kind type of woman, you are strong and bold and you have the most beautiful laugh I've ever heard. I still remember the first day we met and how you smile with so much Joy when you called me. Diaka you have proven to be a real diamond and shine I know you always will. Thank you for standing with me and guiding me and always telling me that you only want my happiness and whatever makes you happy makes me happy and I love you for that. I know that when FGM comes to an end in Sierra Leone your name will be written in the books of history, may you always stand as the voice for the girls who are too afraid to speak up.

Tehsie where do I begin, my cousin, my sister, my best friend and all in all secret keeper. Tehsie we have played together since we were five years old, we have laughed and cried together, we have argued and more than anything we have stood together through the toughest of battles. I have never met anyone who makes me laugh more than you, you always have a way of turning my pain into joy by always reminding me that God is our defender. I am so proud of the woman you have become and I am thankful that I have had you to stand beside me as I have tasted the sweetness and bitterness of the world, you are special Tes and the place you hold in my heart will belong to you forever, I love you always and forever.

Annita Kamara my friend and sister, though life has pulled us apart I wanted to remind you of how grateful I am experiencing the beautiful woman that you are. You are an amazing

woman and a great mother to Josh and Joanna.
I am thankful for the times we could stand
together as mothers when the battles were too
much for us, thank you for all the times you
were there to help me with Gabriella when I
needed support to work. More than thing I pray
that God blesses you endlessly for what you
did for me and Gabriella when no one else
could, I love you and I pray that the fire of love
that God has placed in your heart will never be
blown out.

Hannah Vandy my baby sister you make me so
proud, Edward and Elizabeth Goodwill my
dearest family I love you all more than I can
express, for all your love and kindness you
have shown me during my visits in the states I
am grateful for. I miss you are and I am
grateful to continue to encounter your
greatness.

Fatu Conteh I am so proud of you and I truly
cherish our conversations, the laughter and the
tears and the fact that we can stand united
through it all, you are a great mother to Nasir
and I love how gentle and kind you are; as long
as God is our foundation I am sure that it can
never be broken.

To Mr and Mrs Deen (Haja and Ozee), its true when they say that you could know someone for years and they could not mean well for you but you could meet someone in a short time and they could mean everything to you. My little sister and brother, I am thankful that we were connected and I want to bless you both for standing with me in prayers and comforting me when I needed it. We will be branding in 2019 till the year 3000; I love you both endlessly. #Branding2019

1 WHERE DO I BELONG

I was born on July 20th 1987 in Freetown Sierra Leone at Netland private hospital to Solokor Jehmil Bockari and Baliah Zainab Conteh, from the stories I was told growing up my parents love story wasn't like many that you would hear off. My mother was a divorcee with 4 children from her previous marriage and my father was already married with 3 wives and 3 three children. Not only do I come from a polygamy family but I was born to both Muslim parents and was raised as a Muslim by my father's family who took their faith quite seriously. Earliest and strongest memories have always been about the strong presence of religion in my family and looking back now as an adult I believe that has contributed to my strong foundation and faith in God. As a child I always felt as though I never really understood where I belonged, Some people in my father's family always felt as though I was the child that was too favoured by my father which caused a lot of resentment between me and my father's children. I felt more loved and accepted with my siblings from my mother side, maybe it's because I grew up with them or maybe it's because we slept in the same womb but at times I also felt as though I didn't really belong there either. I was the only one with a different father so I felt as though they had a bond that I could never be apart off and that was really all I ever wanted, to feel accepted and feel like I was a part of someone's story.

They always say that a girl's first love is always her father and I can testify to that statement, my greatest moments that relate to feeling loved all came from memories I shared with my father. I know that my father was not a perfect human and he made his own mistakes but he was such an amazing human being, he was so selfless, so kind, so sweet, funny and so giving; He was my everything. I spent the early years of my life living in between the UK and Sierra Leone with both parents, it was as if when I was separated from one I would yearn for the other but truly I only really yearned for my father most of the time. My mother Zainab aka Baliah was a woman that was made from tough cloth, I remember two sides of my mother when I was younger, there was this tough independent woman who held no prisoners and then there was this other side of her that I remember that was so gentle; though the gentle side I didn't experience so often because she was in the world and needed to keep her mask on. One thing I do clearly remember was her tears, and how often they fell and how often I remember wiping them and telling her that she was going to be okay. I remember the pain I would always feel in my heart when I would see my mother cry, it was as though the entire world was falling apart because if my mother that I saw as this unbreakable warrior was crying then as far as I was concerned something in the world had gone wrong and I was afraid and no longer safe.

After I was born I was told that my mother brought me back to the UK (London) and we settled for a few months before she took me back to my Sierra Leone and left me in the care of her mother and sister, my grandmother (Fatu Sesay) and my Aunty Zainabu my mother's youngest sister. I never understood the bond I had with my Aunty Zainabu growing up, I just always knew that I felt drawn to her until 25 years later when I was told that my Aunty cared for me until I was almost one years old. My mother's other sister Aunty Baby told me stories of how I actually thought that Aunty Zainabu was my mother and I started calling her mama, she said that I was so attached to her that she would have to hide when she had to leave the house. I was told that during the year of me being in Sierra Leone my father would come and see me at my grandmother's house every day after work. My father then was a politician and held a high position which enabled him to look after his children wives and extended family members.

Not Easily Broken

My mother returned to Sierra Leone just
before I turned one and I was told that she
went to her mother's house to see me and
joyfully opened her arms and said " Fatmata
come to mummy, it's me its mummy " and at
that very moment my Aunty Zainabu was just
returning home from the market and as soon as
I saw my Aunty I said " Mama" and ran into her
arms. I was told that my mother packed all my
belongings that day and took me back. My
Aunty B always laughs when she tells me that
story because it just staples who my mother
was, so strong on the outside but had a heart
that would easily melt. I am sure that she
appreciated all the help that my aunt and
grandmother rendered to her in caring for me
but as any mother can testify the most heartbreaking thought would be your child seeing
another woman as their mother because that
highlights the fact that they have transferred
that mother and child bond to someone else
which may be a result of the parents absence.

At the age of 4 I remember my mother moving
us from London to relocate to Manchester
where she believed we would all have a better
family life. For the first few weeks we lived in
a temporary accommodation which were two
sets of two bedroom apartments both facing
each other, my mother, myself and all of my
siblings moved to Manchester together. We
celebrated my 4th birthday during this time and

I remember my cake so clearly, it was a square white and blue cake with four teddy bears lying in bed. At a time when it seemed like our life was unsettled I felt an element of peace, I guess being surrounded by my mother and siblings at that time felt like that was what family was truly about regardless of our circumstances. I can't recall exactly how long we spent in those apartments but I do remember that we were then moved and offered our own house. It was a three bedroom, semi-detached house in Withington Manchester. This was in the early 90's and at that particular time a black and African family moving into a predominately all Caucasian neighbour may not have been the best idea but my mother being who she was fought the battles that would follow without seizing.

I started attending old moat primary school which was just a few minutes away from our house; there I met my two best friend's Liam and Janeane who I built strong bonds with that took us into our teenage years. Liam was my neighbour and his house was opposite mine, we attended the same school and we were the same age so that was the exact recipe for a budding friendship. Our mothers developed this amazing bond and Liam's mother Christine would often babysit me. Christine absolutely loved my mother's cooking especially her special spicy curry. As the years passed and

we settled into our neighbour not everyone
was so accepting of our existence in our new
community. Our family faced many racial
attacks with a lot of the youth often throwing
eggs at our door and sneaking to the back of
our house to spill liquid soap in my mother's
food while she was cooking. My mother grew
tired of the racial attacks and I was told that on
one occasion my mother waited for one of the
boys who would often throw eggs at our door
to come near the house and as he went to
throw the egg my mother opened the door in
few view of the boy's other friend's and
dragged him into the house and shouted that
she would kill him, chop him up into pieces of
meat and cook him. My mother played on their
lack of intelligence and ignorance; these people
use to say that Africans were dirty and that we
ate people. I won't lie and say that I felt sorry
for those boys because they deserved
everything they got at the hands of my mother.

It seemed like the abuse wouldn't stop but my
mother stood strong against those racist bullies
and made sure that her and her children were
safe in that neighbourhood. My mother was
later known as the parent not to be messed
with, that woman was everything, a warrior, a
survivor, a queen; it was almost as though she
had never understood the element of pain. I
didn't understand much about my family
dynamic back then as any 5 year old would but

I remember so clearly the traumatic memories, a lot of those experiences didn't make much sense to me because I was just a child that was growing up in what I classed as a normal family. My mother was a single mother and I was the fifth and last child. The eldest of us was Abdul, then Rakie, Rashida, Lamin and then me, Abdul the first born is so full of wisdom, he is so optimistic even when he speaks of his painful experiences. Whenever I struggled with the absence of my father in my life my brother Abdul seemed to always fill that void back then. Rakie being the second born has always been the one that kept the family together, the mother of us all who was so brave and so funny with a heart that was bigger than the ocean but sometimes seemed to be so afraid of her own strength but I would put that down to so much of the bitterness she had to taste in her childhood. Rakie taught me a lot about resilience, she pushed me so hard to fight against the odds that wanted to break me but where so much brokenness exist the peace is stolen and during our storms of life we were separated. Rashida was the sibling that is different, I spent my entire childhood trying to understand her and every time I thought I did I would realise that I didn't. I finally understood who she was after I became a mother because only then could I understand that my sister struggled with so much that our culture was never ready to accept and as a

mother I was able to then step into my
mother's shoes and realise that she made
mistakes that affected the bond between her
and her children. Rashida is one of the most
ambitious people I know, she puts her mind to
something and she achieves it. I don't think
I've ever witnessed her fail at anything I just
know that growing up I didn't like her very
much because she seemed to be so tough on
me. Rakie was different, Rakie mothered me
and Rashida pushed me; I didn't need to be
pushed I needed to be mothered and Rakie had
that balance which is why our relationship
always seemed to be stronger. I won't take
anything good away from Rashida, we had
great moments and memories, as unsettled as
our relationship has always been I can say that
when she wanted to be a sister she could be
the best sister I could ever dream off.
Sometimes it just felt as though she wanted me
to be more like her and I wasn't like her at all,
I was and always wanted to be me.

Rashida trained as an Air hostess and got her
first job with Virgin Atlantic, Richard Branson
gave her; her flying wings and till this day I
remember how proud everyone in our family
was of her. The first time I saw my sister in
her uniform I can remember how proud I felt
and in my heart I said " that is my big sister ".
She is so beautiful and well put together, she
took so much pride in her appearance and was

so good and what she did. Rashida went on to
work for many other airlines in managerial
roles and later worked for private airlines
flying royalty and celebrities like Mariah
Carey. When it came to career development
she had that down and never struggled in that
area. Lamin was the typical boy of the family,
full of laughter, loved life and tends to live in
the moment. Our bond was normal; I think our
relationship was the only one that seemed
normal when I related it to the rest of the
world. We had our normal sibling fights and
arguments as; he would tease me and make me
so angry that on one occasion I slammed my
room door on his finger. At the age of sixteen
Lamin went into the British army after he gave
our mother a few reasons to consider sending
him back home to Sierra Leone permanently.
Lamin did very well in the army I still
remember the ceremony we attended when he
was officially a soldier of the British army. My
mother and my step father Uncle Akie were so
proud of him as was I because indeed I was so
happy to see my brother serving his country
and being so proud to do it. Lamin went on to
do great things in the British Army, he became
Sergeant Deen and also spent some time as
Queen guard at Buckingham palace. He did also
take advantage of his new title by threatening
the guys in our neighbour that none of them
were allowed to date me, I only found this out
after I thought I fell in love with one of them

and as we both talked and liked each other he confided in my best friend Leah that he could never date me because my brother had threatened them all that they are not allowed to go near me. At the time I was very angry because all I saw was that my brother was trying to stand in my way of happiness, and it worked because none of the guys would even look at me. My friend Leah found that to be so funny but as time went on and I grew up he became more protective and I just realised that it was actually sweet so I decided to start liking guys that lived outside my neighbourhood to save myself the heartache.

My mother seemed to manage looking after us all at the time, although I was the youngest and my older siblings were old enough to look after themselves. My mother had been a qualified nurse, worked with social services and was a teacher in her young years in the UK but later chose the path of business. She was a market trader and worked in most of the markets in Manchester that's how she took care of us. My Mother also travelled a lot between the USA, Gambia and Sierra Leone where she would buy and sell a lot of her goods which consisted of food and clothing products. I remember one particular night I think was still five or maybe six years old but I remember my mother doing a lot of packing as she was preparing to ship some things to Sierra Leone and there was lots

of boxes and tape and for some reason our
lights were off but there was a lot of candles
around the house. It was me, my mum, Rashida
and Lamin at home at the time, I saw Lamin
and Rashida whispering in a corner and a few
moments later they called me and told me they
wanted to play a game with me. I agreed and to
my surprise I was stripped naked, wrapped in
brown trap and they put me outside the back
garden and locked the door. I couldn't move
because my entire body was taped together
and so was my mouth. It was cold and windy
and tears were rolling down my cheeks
because I started to realise that I didn't like the
game. I was there for a little while but I could
hear my mother inside the house panicking
trying to find me and shouting my name and
after a while the back door opened and my
mother stood there in entire shock and
shouted, she pulled me quickly into the house
and started pulling the tape away from me as I
cried and she tried to get me warm. My mother
was so furious, she put my clothes back on and
wrapped me with a blanket so my system
would warm up quicker. Rashida and Lamin
definitely received a good dose of punishment I
just can't remember what it was but I do
remember my mother's screams and
statements of their cruel act towards
me. When I look back at that incident now I
don't hold any grudges towards them, one thing
about our family is that we are very playful and

may be that was a joke that they took way too far but I am sure if they remember it they will regret it. This was the first of many traumatic incidents in my life that fortunately taught me about how resilient I am and how much of a forgiving and peaceful nature that I possess. My siblings became the first learning point in which I would learn about life the hardest way not because they hated me or didn't love me but because that's how they experienced it.

2 TWO WORLDS APART
(THE SISTER WIVES)

I can't remember what day it was or what month or even the year, I just remember that it was winter and it was extremely cold. I ran around Heathrow airport and played while Rakie and my mother spoke to the check-in attendants. I was a six year old with a sassy mouth and a wild imagination and on this particular day everything seemed like a normal day to me. I even remember me and my mother's journey to London from Manchester, we took the national express coach and stopped over in Birmingham, I can't recall much but I can remember how cold the weather was. I stood at the airport and I clearly remember my mother's posture changing, she became emotional and I could sense that she was fighting so hard to hold back her tears. A beautiful Caucasian Air Hostess walked over to us but stood just a little distance away and my mother bent down on her knees and pulled me closer, she said "Fatmata Mummy loves you very much okay "I didn't understand so I just stared at her blankly and she continued to profess her love for me and she hugged me and I looked over at my sister Rakie and saw tears streaming down her face and I still didn't understand what was happening. A few moments later the air hostess walked over to me and introduced herself to me with a calm and comforting voice and reached out her hand for me to hold her which I did because I still couldn't make sense of what was happening. The air hostess took my hand and lead me away from my mother and sister and I walked with her towards this big two barrel grey door and I kept glancing back at my mother and sister to see if they would follow us but I saw them weeping. Rakie was embracing my mother as she cried and as we entered the double barrel grey door I walked in and stopped and looked back at my mother crying bitterly and the hostess rubbing my hands as a sense of comfort. I stood as the doors closed and the hostess started pulling me away and I could still see my mother and sister through the glass opening of the doors and then I lost it, I started crying and screaming because then somehow I knew that I was being separated from my mother and I just didn't understand why. What had I done, where was I going; my mind was spinning and I saw another hostess run towards us as they both attempted to calm me down, the second hostess carried me and I lay my head on her shoulder as I cried for my mother.

We got onto the plane and they took me to my seat and straight away all of the attendants came over to introduce themselves to me, I think it was a way of them distracting me from what was happening. I looked out the window and noticed I was on a plane and then I started crying again, I wasn't sitting far from the plane door so I kept my eyes focused on the door hoping that at any moment my mother and sister would walk in and either take me back or seat next to me but they didn't. I watched as one of the flight attendants approached the door and slowly closed it and there it was, the reality of what I was dreading, I was being taken away and throughout that whole process I kept telling myself that at some point my mother or sister would walk in and take me back and that flight door closing felt like a hammer on my heart. Tears continued to roll down my cheeks as I frantically looked through all the windows of the plane for a sign that my mother was coming. The pilot started making his announcements and the plane's engine was on and as the engine went louder so did the sound of my cries as I called out for my mummy. The plane started to move and I went straight into panic mode and started frantically looking around through the windows and up and down the aisles and straight away the air hostess that was responsible for me rushed over and sat right next me fastened her seat belt and embraced me into a tight hug as she comforted me and kept telling me "it's going to be okay precious, everything is going to be just fine ". As the plane went into the air I started having flash backs of the events that occurred a few months before. The images of my mother packing boxes and empty suitcases on the bedroom floor and then the last image of my mother's face as they pulled me away from her at the airport. My heart felt so heavy I couldn't make sense of what was happening to me and what I was about to face I just knew that I was afraid. The tiredness from all the crying knocked me out and by the time I woke up I was given food to eat and it was time for the plane to land, the air hostess did her best to settle me and keep me in good spirits. When it was time for the plane to land she got me prepared and took me to the crew and the pilots to say goodbye. The plane doors opened and I was hit by a wave of heat that was ridiculous, it was dark but I remember the sight of palm trees at Lungi airport. As we walked off the plane with the air hostess holding my hand tightly I looked around and saw all these black faces, it was a cultural shock at first because I was pulled out of an environment where apart from my immediate family 80% of the people I engaged with were Caucasian, I attended a primary school that seemed as though every class needed one black face to make up for the demographic statistics of inclusion. As we entered the airport I just remember how busy it was, so many travellers and yet again I was being taken into the unknown. We approached a tall dark skinned man who wore grey trousers and a cream lose shirt, he rushed out to us and introduced himself, he was one of the airport staff. The air hostess bent down to my level and told me that it was time for me to go and wished me a safe journey, she told me that I was going to be okay and that this lovely man would take me to my family. Tears started to fill my eyes again and she touched my cheek and told me not be afraid that I was going to be just fine and she gave me a tight hug as she handed me over to the man with the cream shirt with my hand luggage and my passport, some papers and she

smiled as she waved and turned away and
walked back towards the plane.

The man with the cream shirt took my hand
and as we walked he said "Fatmata welcome
home "and he smiled, I looked up at him with
my teary eyes and looked back at the direction
that we were walking. As we walked we came
to a standstill as another man came running
over and said "The Pa dai cam insai, e dai cam
now "this in English meant that he was on his
way, his coming now, moments later I saw this
man wearing this check shirt pushing his way
through a crowd of people that were
desperately fighting for his attention as they
greeted him. He continued to push through and
he got nearer with two or three people walking
beside him I just remember how handsome he
was, I was taken aback by his appearance,
there was something about him and straight
away something in that moment where I felt
alone and lost started to make spiritual sense.
The man in the check shirt was well dressed
and smelt so good, he approached us with an
excited look in his eyes and he quickly greeted
the man in the cream shirt who seemed excited
to also see the man in the check shirt. He bent
down and looked me in the eyes and said "
Fatmata it's me, it's daddy " I burst into tears
and he grabbed and stood up and placed my
head on his shoulder as I cried. He laughed and

31

told the airport staff that I was in shock and missing my mother. I never had any memories of my father before this moment I just know that instantly I fell in love with him, he was so gentle and held me like a raw egg that he didn't want to ever break. We got into the car and made our way to what would my new home, I remember the first memory I created of my father was that he was a man of great character; throughout our journey on the way home so many people came begging him for money and thanking him for one favour or another and I remember that there was not one person that asked that he didn't give. We went on the ferry to cross the Lungi River and my father kept me in his arms, I refused to allow anyone else to touch me at this point. I decided that since I had just lost my mother I needed to hold on to the only parent that was present. The place was dark but we drove and got to a big bungalow house, when the car door opened there were so many faces, people that I didn't know all shouting my name and wanting to touch me but I remember just gripping my dad really tight until we entered the house. Once the lights were turned on and the living room was full of faces that I didn't recognise and soon enough my father started to introduce me to my family. First I met my elder brother Borboh who was really handsome; he was really dark skinned with beautiful skin like chocolate. Then there was my elder sister

Musu, she looked just like my brother and they both hugged me and said how much I had grown. My dad then introduced me to his two wives, who both commented on how big I was, they were both living in the same house, and they were to be my step-mothers. The house was full of family members, immediate and extended, cousins, uncles, aunties and their children. I came to realise that I came from a very big family and my father had a huge responsibility to take care of them all.

That night I slept in my father's bed with him and one of his wives and I spent the entire night on his chest like a little baby, it made me forget the pain of what had just happened to me. The next morning I woke up to more visitors, I came out of the room holding my father's hand and hiding my face behind his pasture. The first thing I saw was the sunshine, the sun was shining so bright and it was beautiful. There was this beautiful big mango tree right in front of our house and it was so big that it almost looked like a house of its own and you could sit under it for shade away from the sunshine. My father introduced me to two people that would be important figures in my life during this time, my grandmother my father's mother Hawa Kamara and my father's first born daughter Hawa Bockari. My sister Hawa was so happy to see me, she carried me and kept telling me how much I looked like her and our father and indeed she was right the three of us looked so much like it was almost unreal. My grandmother did not spoke krio properly and spoke no English but she was the pillar of our family, my grandmother was so nurturing and loved her children so much, she had three sons Solokor Bockari (My father) Abu Bockari and Francis Bockari (My Uncles).

My grandmother lived five minutes away from my father's house in my Uncle Abu's house and next door to my Uncle Abu's house my Uncle Francis lived there with his wife and children. Looking back now our family was so unified in how the family lived, the three brothers no matter how many times they had their misunderstandings they had this bond that was hard to understand. Solokor, Abu and Francis three men who were not born into riches but worked so hard to be educated and every step of the way took their family along on the road to success. My father and his brothers loved their mother so much, she seemed to be apple of their eyes and my grandmother "Mama Hawa" as everyone called her was very family orientated, she was the peace marker. She was the type of woman that loved the unloved and helped those in need even if it meant using her last penny. I can remember the countless times when I would go to my grandmother's room and go under her bed and eat her powdered milk and other provisions that her sons had given her. She would start shouting and off course every time that my father or uncles would replace the supplies I would repeat the same pattern, that was my grandmother and I enjoyed playing hide and seek under her bed and the food was a bonus.

My father spent a lot of time at work, the first few months was hard for me to adjust to the changes of my environment. There was this terrible vibe in our house between both of my step-mothers, I remember clearly that one of my step-mothers was my main care provider; she looked after me on a daily washing and feeding me. Only one of my father's wives had children for him which was my siblings Musu and Borboh, Hawa the first born was from my father's first marriage to Hawa's mother Aunty Taibi. At the time I was the last child but with my father's job, influence and financial capability came more children born to girlfriends he had away from his marriages. My father had two children after me, my younger brother Borboh and sister JJ. My father's extra marital affairs caused a lot of discomfort with his wives at home with each one competing to be the wife in charge but each time they came to the realisation that their control was limited as long as my father continued to have outside interest. The world where it seemed like people were forever fighting to be the centre of my father's world, I received his attention so freely. There was something about our bond that was unique, he could never hide the fact that I was his favourite and that caused a lot of jealousy with some of my siblings because it appeared that there was nothing that I would ask for from my father that I wouldn't get, even if the first response was no I would just need to sit on his lap and cry and he would get angry and that no would turn into a fast yes. Did my father hate to see me cry or was I just his weakness. I remember a time when I called my father and asked him if I was a mistake, my father was appalled and asked me why I asked such a question, I told him it was because it seemed like I was lost in a world where there seemed to be so many children and I was one of many. My father laughed and explained to me that he actually asked my mother to bore a child for him and my mother gave him me, this melted my heart and made me feel extra special. On many nights I would sit down at the veranda of our house way past my bedtime waiting for my father to come home from work, some days I would be lucky and he would come home with ice cream, popcorn and other treats for me and other nights I would cry myself to sleep because he wouldn't come home at all. I don't know who felt worst me or his wives. I slept in the same room with my dad and one of wives so most nights it would just be me and my step-mother in the bed. I am sure we both had the same anxiety of wondering where he was but my heart was aching for the treats and daddy's love that I didn't get while I am very sure my step-mother's heart ached for a total different reason. A time came when I started to feel my step-mother's pain, I felt so sorry for her because there she was this wife that did everything for her husband, she had to share him with the other wife in the house that she constantly had fights with and then having to share him with girlfriends that would have children for him that they would hand over to her to nurture and each time she obliged, I often wondered how any woman could accept so much but this was west African cultural, a high percentage men who would claim to be happily married would openly have girlfriends outside the marital home that the wives were fully aware off. In many cases with Islamic families like mine these girlfriends would later become wives as soon as it was apparent that the woman was with child, I am sure this is how a lot of women secured marriage with men they were aware already had family commitments.

It seemed like the more my father's success came the further he was away from his wives and was more of the world's property, I didn't feel the pressure as much because whenever my dad was home I got most of his attention, I was beside him at all times. There was an emotional strain on me once I started school,

the pressure of the change of environment
started to reflect in my communication and in
my learning, I hardly spoke to people that I
didn't know in school only my siblings and
cousins that attended the same school and
these concerns were expressed to my father
and step-mothers. My mother called a few
times a month, I patiently waited for those calls
for the first few months that's all I looked
forward too but there was a part of me that
was so angry at her, every time she would call
I would ask her the same question " Mummy
when am I coming back home " And every time
she would give me the same reply "soon
Fatmata" after a year passed I stopped asking,
instead I just enjoyed our telephone calls and
accepted that for that present moment I had my
father and until she was ready I would remain
in my father's arms. During this time some
many things started to come to light and the
one thing that was very evident was the
jealousy between my father's children on the
basis of who got what and who he seemed to
show more favour. While the rift between the
siblings started so did the rift between his
wives. My father was re-positioned from
Freetown to another city in Sierra Leone called
BO and when it was time for my father to go he
took one of his wives along (Aunty Musu) who
was my main carer. I cried a lot because I
knew there would be major changes with my
father not being around and now being left in

the hands of my father's other wife (Aunty Hannah) who everyone known not to be the nicest of people compared to Aunty Musu. Aunty Musu was more nurturing, she was raised in the village so she had different principles about family life whereas Aunty Hannah was a Freetown raised woman who knew about the streets, she was more exposed to a lot of things and wasn't the type of woman that stood beside or behind her husband. she seemed to want to run her own show; while my father strayed with his extra marital affairs there was always rumours that she had a few of her own.

My Father promised that we could go and stay with him in BO every time we had school holidays and indeed he kept to his promise. Being the children of a politician we got certain privileges, during these times there was airspace in a place called Hastings in Freetown and flights operated from Freetown to BO city, this was a service that was limited to those that could afford whatever the cost was. This was my father's treat for me and my siblings every time we had a holiday from school. Our house in BO was so beautiful; it sat on this hill and stood on a big land. My cousins and I would run freely in the summer breeze while Aunty Musu would spend her entire day in the kitchen cooking to entertain my father's political guests. I remember a very sunny day while I was playing in the back of the house alone running around and my father sat at the side of the house with his guest and my father called me and said "Fatmata come here "I ran over and sat on his lap as his guest commented on how much I looked like my father and my father as always laughed and replied that I was his twin. My father held something in his hand that was wrapped in a tissue and he unwrapped it and showed it to me and it glittered and sparkled and there it was a diamond, as real as they come and as raw. I held the diamond in my hand for a few moments before returning it to my father's palms, I didn't realise it then but later on in life it occurred to me that I had held something so precious.

All our time spent in BO was filled with positive memories except on one particular trip there were rumours that my father was dating someone that my step-mum Aunty Musu knew and this caused great discomfort for her. I remember that day so clearly my father didn't sleep at home the previous day and when he returned Aunty Musu was not in the best of moods. I slept in the same bed as my father and step-mother and their room was an end-suite room so my father walked into the room and I got up from the bed and jumped into his arms, he kissed me and hugged me tightly. Aunty Musu told me to go and brush my teeth so I went into the bathroom and she closed the door behind me. While I was brushing my teeth I heard noise coming from the bedroom and the noise became louder and I realised that they were arguing. I finished brushing my teeth and opened the door to go back into the room and was met with the horrifying scene of Aunty Musu pointing a gun at my father and screaming at him to tell her where he was last night. I immediately screamed and ran and stood in front of my father and shouted "Please don't shoot my dad please "my father tried to push me back into the bathroom but I refused as they continued to argue and my father urged her to put the gun down. I ran over to the balcony of the room and shouted down to my cousin Abu that was outside and told him what was happening. Abu and some of my other cousins came rushing upstairs but when they tried open the door it was locked and they shouted for me to open the door and at this time my father had taken the gun from Aunty Musu and they were physically fighting. I ran over to the door frantically trying to open it and realised that Aunty Musu had locked the door with a key, I told Abu that the door was locked with a key as I continued to cry and shout for help. My cousins had to kick the door down and separate my dad and Aunty Musu, one of my cousins quickly carried me and rushed me out of the room while they settled the incident.

Not Easily Broken

My father left the house and Aunty Musu was being comforted by her family, I sat in the room with Abu who then had the gun in his possession and I asked him what it was and he told me that it was something dangerous and no one in the house should have it. He wrapped it up and reassured me that everything was okay; this was the first time that I saw evidence of Aunty Musu's pain. She always seemed so unbothered by my father's extra marital affairs but there was something about this particular woman that seemed to hit her hard and I guess she wanted to go against the label she had been given as the soft wife that accepted everything and never spoke up. Her actions spoke very loudly but it was too late because that relationship resulted in another one of my father's children which I know may have been another bitter pill to swallow for his wives.

3 SILENT TEARS

I hated the idea of returning back to return to
Aunty Hannah's care because I knew what that
meant for me. It seemed as though when my
father wasn't around everyone showed their
true colors, they did what they wanted because
there was nobody to tell them otherwise and
everyone was living in fear of Aunty Hannah so
no one dared to speak against her to my father.
When she wanted to be nice she was nice but
she was known as the step-mother and wife
that no one really liked because she did a lot of
things that made everyone question her
motives. I remember many times when I would
get asked to leave school because she wouldn't
pay my school fees, I went to a private school
and when my father would send our monthly
allowances she would use it to live her own
luxury lifestyle which everyone in the family
witnessed but no one was brave enough to
speak up. On many occasions my Uncles would
step-up and meet our needs but I just never
understood why they never spoke to their
brother about what was going on.

Things became very intense between me and

my elder sister Musu at the house; it was
almost as though she unmasked herself and
revealed to me a level of hate that I hadn't
seen before. There were countless times when
she would purposely do something so wicked
and lie and tell her mother Aunty Hannah that it
was me and I would get beaten mercilessly. On
one particular occasion Aunty Hannah beat me
so bad that I ran to my grandmother's house
with wounds and I remember Mama Hawa
crying and calling her neighbors to be a
witness. My grandmother stated that maybe
Aunty Hannah wanted to beat me to death
because that wasn't the first time it had
happened. Mama Hawa cleaned me up and I
stayed with her for a few days. Nothing made
my sister Musu happier than the times when I
would get in trouble, I knew that her issues
steamed from the jealousy that she felt
because of me and my father's bond but
brother Borboh wasn't like that at all, he was
so kind and loved me so much. He was the first
son so he enjoyed most of the privileges of my
father's success. We called him Number 1
because of the amount of boys in our family
with the same name Borboh. My brother was
the first born son from all the brothers so he
got our grandfather's name (Borboh Bockari),

Not Easily Broken

My brother had access to my father's money and cars so as much as the success came so did my brother's downfall because a point came when neither my father or my brother's mother Aunty Hannah could control his behavior anymore.

Living in that house started feeling like a nightmare, I often used the time I spent with my grandmother and cousins as a getaway knowing that when I returned home I was at risk of falling into Satan's trap. Musu's hate for me only seemed to grow and I couldn't make sense of what is what that I had done. Some days she would look at me with this deep rooted anger almost like my existence tormented her. Another year passed and it seemed like my father was further away from me than I could reach, the novelty of being the youngest child and the apple of my father's eye had worn off and everyone in that house started treating me however they pleased. I remember so many days when I would sit in the living room hoping that the phone would ring and it would be my mother, I really wanted to go back home because my father wasn't around and neither was Aunty Musu who at the time was taking good care of me. It started to feel like I was living in a repeated pattern of abandonment and I felt a strong sense of rejection.

There was one particular night that I remember so clearly, it was really hot and most days I would sleep on the mattress on the floor with nothing but my top and underwear on. I was sleeping and I felt this weight over me, it was heavy and it felt like I was in a deep sleep fighting to wake up and the whole time I fought the sleep and the weight off this heavy human that was holding me down. I was so powerless, I don't know if was shock or whether I couldn't get up but by the time I finally did all I felt was the wetness in my vagina and my underwear at my ankles. This was just before my 7th birthday and I remember this because after my birthday it happened again and again and again and every time I promised myself that I would open my eyes in time to see his face. I spent a lot of time trying to make sense of what was happening to me, was this normal and why anyone couldn't notice what was happening, some nights I would stay awake really late tossing and turning on my mattress to scare him away because he would know I was awake and wouldn't come in; other nights I would be so tired that I would fall asleep and he would come in and rape me. Months went by and my behavior changed, I talked less and became withdrawn and no one at home noticed but I remember that my school teacher noticed because she spoke to Aunty Hannah about it during a parents meeting at school but my step-mother didn't care much because she was busy enjoying her freedom and ultimate control of the household.

Soon enough I started hating night time because I knew well what that meant for me, if I could stay awake long enough he would try to come into the room and realise that I was awake I would see his shadow turning back and returning to the lounge. One night I promised myself that I would stay alert long enough so that I could see his face so that I would know who was doing this to me. I lay down with my eyes closed pretending to be asleep and off course he came into the room, Aunty Musu was home from BO this time and she as fast asleep on the bed that her and my father shared with her back turned away from me. He came in and clamed on top of me and took my underwear off, my heart was beating so fast and I just wanted to scream, I wanted to bite him or kick him but the one emotion I felt at that moment was fear. He started to rape me and silently I cried from the inside as my invisible tears fell and then I decide to move my body and he jumped up and was tip toeing out the room and I quickly opened my eyes and got up and just in time I got a glimpse of my abuser, my heart fell and I felt sick to my stomach and I started to cry as I lay back down and had flashbacks of all the other nights he had raped me and the shadow of his face that I had not seen so clearly but this night it was clear enough because of the shorts he wore and his signature bald head; my abuser was no other than my uncle, my father's youngest brother Solokor who was living with us at the time.

A cousin from another city came to stay with us for a while and we had grown really close, she was older than me but she was like the sister I needed at the time. She made me laugh and made me forget about what had been happening to me. While she stayed with us and the room was full he wouldn't come in at night so for a while I was safe. I confided in my cousin about what was going on and she urged me to tell Aunty Musu about it and I told her that I was scared and she promised that she would come with me to tell her. We went to the back of our house where Aunty Musu was cooking and doing laundry and my cousin sat down near her and told her that there is something she needed to tell her and Aunty Musu asked what it was and my cousin explained to her what I had told her, her face changed and she looked shocked but continued with what she was doing as she asked me some questions which I answered. Till this present moment I can never understand why she seemed so unbothered about abuse, it didn't seem to bother her it was almost as though it was something that was just accepted because I had heard many family stories of similar cases in which cousins who spoke out against their abusers were alienated and casted out of the family and labeled as liars because a lot of the men that were doing the abusing were the bread winners for the family and I am guessing a child's innocence is not as important as living a sustainable life.

My life seemed as though it was just getting from bad to worse, I was dealing with being sexually abused by my Uncle, emotionally abused by my sister and physically abused by my step-mother. Where did I go wrong, my step-mother Aunty Hannah seemed to be so far gone in her acts of wickedness that she extended her anger towards me many times. She treated her daughter Musu just as any mother would treat her child; she was the apple of her eye and couldn't do any wrong in her eyes. She would always wedge war between Musu and our eldest sister Hawa because Aunty Hannah had an issue with every other child that my father had that wasn't her children. She came across so bitter at times it was almost like she hated us. Hawa lived with her mother but the opportunities that I would get to spend time with her was always so refreshing, spending time with Hawa was like being with my Dad again, it was that special bond, a genuine love. I was a child that was so young but was carrying so much pain, rage and sorrow in my tiny little heart.

I started displaying a lot of rage and everyone classed me as a spoilt brat, they said when I don't get want I want I act out,I would get so angry and I would go into my father's room and throw everything around and pull suitcases down and rip clothes apart and just scream. No one ever thought to ask why I was so angry but I have come to understand that people can see

and identify pain but they just do not have what
it takes to strip away those hard layers to see
what's underneath the bricks. I was so angry, I
was angry at my mother and my father and I
was angry at myself because I felt as though
something had to be wrong with me for me to
keep having these issues were people are
beating me and raping me and telling lies on
me and abandoning me. I made myself believe
that I was the problem and many times as
young as I was I just wished that I wasn't alive
anymore because death would have been
better than living the life that I was living
without any protection or anyone that was
there continuously reassuring me that I was
loved. I hated him with every breathe that was
inside of me, every time I would see this grown
man walking around our family and most days
parading his girlfriend around it made me sick,
I wished that I was an adult so that I could have
a voice to speak and they would hear me;
living in that house felt like I was living as a
person on mute at times. I played like a child
and sometimes laughed like a child and if you
looked at me you would see a child but my soul
and heart had matured and surpassed my age.

The local kids around our area had their bondo

celebration, in the western world this is called the FGM practice, FGM during those times was normality and a lot of families forcefully performed the practice on their female children with promises of them later having this big party to celebrate them becoming a woman. Our step-mothers started having discussions about all the girls in the house being put into bondo, I had heard stories about what they do in there and how they cut girls and how the girls bleed so I had already had a huge fear of this. I remember speaking to my mother on the phone one day and crying to her that I was afraid because I had heard that my step-mother wanted to put us through it and I told my mother that my dad wasn't around and I was scared. My mother contacted my father and expressed those concerns to

him and through whispers in the household I later heard that my father sent a message to his wives that if any one of them touches his children and puts them forward for FGM he would physically kill them. His wives honored what he said but one of them stated that when they were ready for us they would put us into the FGM society without my father's permission and there would be nothing he could do about it because it would be too late. I started living with that fear of wondering when my turn would be, whenever I would hear that a Sowai (The Head of the FGM society) was around our area I would leave home and go and spend the entire day with my grandmother or other friends where no one could find me. I lived in fear of so many times and some of those things I had no control over but I promised myself that I would do whatever it took to keep myself safe from my womanhood being cut wasn't my innocence being taken enough. Everyone used to say that I was this sharp mouthed young girl who spoke about whatever she felt and held no prisoners, sometimes I was so full of life especially the time when my Uncle was no longer around much, I think he started studying or working but I just know that I was relieved that he was no longer around the house as much and this meant I could sleep a little more peacefully at night but if I am truly honest as he stole away my innocence he also stole away my peace to sleep and no matter how deeply I slept if I heard the sound of a creaking door opening or a pin dropping I would wake up immediately, that was my way of fighting back by waking up sooner.

It's amazing what pain can open your eyes to
see, after swallowing that bitter pill of sexual
abuse I also started noticing that a lot of the
other young girls that I played with were in the
same situation as me. I noticed how when we
would be playing and their Uncle or older
cousin would come over and it was how they
were touched or spoken too that made me
suspicious. It was that sick perverted look in
their eyes and the look of shame in the girl's
eyes that made me know what was happening
because I too knew that look of shame because
I carried it with me often. There was a young
girl that I use to play with and one day we
were playing hide and seek in this half built
house and there was a lot of us and me and her
were partners, we played a few rounds and
then suddenly she went missing and I looked
for her everywhere and then finally I stumbled
upon a horrific sight, she was pressed against
the wall by some building bricks while her
older male cousin who was at least 15 at the
time was raping her. Just like me she stood
there frozen with emptiness in her eyes and
her underwear at her ankles; I ran away and
found a corner to cry it out because just like
me she was only 8 years old. A few days later
when we played together again I asked if her

cousin had ever touched her in a bad way and she looked down to the ground as we both sat down and played with stones and she told me that he does things to her that she doesn't like but she can't say anything because no one will believe her and in that moment I saw myself and I bonded with her on another level. I felt the need to protect her from him; I told myself that no one protected me so I would protect her. He would always find ways to get her alone by calling her in his room to get something or cornering her in dark places when no adults are around so I started being around her more often and whenever he would call her I would go along and he would find ways to get me to leave but I never left and I know that irritated him but I made a vow to myself and I was going to protect my friend even if I could only do that for her on weekends and Holidays when I was able to play with her.

I did my best to live my life like a normal 8 year old trying hard to erase all the things that had happened to me, I lived with the good and accepted whatever bad was given to me. There were moments that were good and most of those moments I remember sharing with my father, grandmother and cousins. It's hard to highlight all the wonderful memories when the bitter memories caused so much damage, I became the love child of my parents that was always waiting for either my mother or father to step up and remove me from that environment. An experience that was suppose to mould me positively and install great cultural values inside of me instead broke me, stole from me and gave me a bitter taste of the world that made it hard for me to relate to the rest of the world properly. I witnessed what I didn't want in a marriage and how I didn't want to be as a woman through what I saw both of my step-mothers doing, they were both so different but I could also sense that they both somehow lacked what I think my father needed in wives to keep him focused on the goals he needed to achieve for himself but instead their selfishness and greed pushed him further away into the arms of the world that was ready to use and abuse the platform he had been given for their own selfish desires.

My Father would come home from BO once in a while and spend the weekends with us, those moments I valued a lot because I started to feel like I was losing my father to the world of politics. Everything was about his work and what needed to be done for the outside world and he didn't even know that his family was severely broken and his daughter was being violated in the worst way possible. Whenever my father didn't have time to fit us into his schedule he would give my cousin Abu a stack of cash and Abu and our driver would take us to any supermarket of our choice and we would buy whatever we wanted. The love my father showed us didn't change it was still the same, it was just his focus that seemed to shift but I understood it because this man was responsible for so many people in his family that he had to pay house rent for, college fees and general living expenses. My father was indeed the king of his castle, he was the man that never ran away from his responsibilities but always faced them head on until he found a solution. I don't remember a time when my father was around that he could actually just lay down in bed and just rest or just have time for his private thoughts because there were always people coming to our house. Some of them came asking for favors, help with jobs, help with money to pay their children's school fees and my father being who he was I never witnessed him turning anyone away because

most of those times when he was home I was
right beside him sitting on his lap or near
enough to jump and hug him whenever I
wanted. I became the pawn that my family
used whenever they wanted something from
my father, it was known that if my father could
say no to anyone else she couldn't say no to
FA and on many occasions when my sister
Musu wanted something from my father that
she knew she couldn't get she would call me to
a corner and be really nice and gentle and
plead with me to go and ask my father for what
she wanted but I had to pretend it was for me.
She was good at using people to get what she
wanted, she manipulated very well and knew
how to play with people's emotions for her own
benefit, and she was indeed her mother's
daughter. She had everything that she ever
wanted but it just never seemed to be enough
for her because she always wanted more, to be
more popular and have everything that all the
other rich girls in school had and whether my
father liked it or not he would give it to her but
after all they were born into riches, they met a
father who could give them the best of the
best. My father wasn't so lucky and didn't grow
up with such privileges. The Bockari brothers
Solokor, Francis and Abu didn't have the best

of starts in life but they were loved and disciplined and they held each other's hands as they fought their way out of the boundaries that held them down and knocked on the doors of accomplishment and success.

My father was such an honorable man, I am yet to meet a person that had anything negative to say about him, he was so well educated and well groomed, he took a lot of pride in his appearance and his smile could light up every room. Without realising he was the first man I ever fell in love with because he showed me love at a level that was hard for most men to reach. The flame of love that he set in my heart is what helped me carry the weight of the pain that was trying to weigh me down because every time I would get angry and have flash backs around those torturing nights I would also see my father's face, I would hear his laughter and something inside of me would tell me to fight the narrative that all men are veil creatures because it was a man that violated me, a man I trusted that took away my innocence and I should have hated all men but my father's love fought those ideals and I couldn't bring myself to place that blame on the men of universe. I found a wooden box and I tore my chest open, took my heart out and wiped away the darkness that my abuser put there, my rage and my pain, I poured that pain into that wooden box and I swallowed it because I knew there was no room for me to cry or to scream; so for now I had to accept that my story was mute but something inside of me reassured me that one day no matter how long it takes I would vomit that box out and break it apart and free myself from the pain of holding in my rage but until then I would allow the world to tell me why I was angry and try to heal the wounds that they cannot see.

4 THE REFUGEE ON THE SHORE OF GAMBIA

In 1996 the rebel war seemed to intensify and
nothing or no one was safe, I remember one
visit we had in BO and on this particular night
my father didn't sleep at home and we were all
fast asleep and I was woken up by the noise of
people shouting and the sound of footsteps up
and down the stairs. I woke up and realised
Aunty Musu wasn't in the bed next to me, I got
out of the bed and walked out of my father's
room and stood by the stairs and I could
clearly hear the loud voices of people rushing.
I walked down the stairs and stood still and
watched the chaos that was my family running
in and out the house packing their belongings, I
was shocked and didn't understand what was
happening and then someone told me to put
some shoes on, I rushed up the stairs in panic
and slid my feet into what seemed like my
father's giant slippers and came back
downstairs and started looking for Aunty Musu.
A group of villagers from a nearby village
came running by our housing and shouting "
Dem dai cam oh dem dai cam " which meant

that they were coming and they were on their
way, the rebels who started the civil war in
Sierra Leone. The panic increased and one of
my Uncles' instructed that everyone leave
whatever was in the house and get into the
cars straight away so we could drive to the
centre of BO city where we would be safe. It
was no secret that when the rebels attack they
aim government workers/ministers and their
children so there was a huge panic for our
safety especially because then it was clear
knowledge that we were in town holidaying
with our father.

My cousin Abu grabbed me and carried me as
we all rushed into the cars and as we left our
drive way and turned onto the main street we
looked behind we saw them from afar on foot
running, it was only by God's grace because if
we would have delayed leaving ten minutes
later I may not be alive to tell this story. The
car was speeding and someone was able to get
in touch with my father and he made
arrangements for a safe house for us to spend
the night which was one of his friends. It was
hard to fall asleep that night because there was
so much panic in the city and all I remember
was just hoping that my Father was okay and

that where ever he was that he wouldn't be placed under any harm. We slept off and woke up in the morning in my father's friend's house, he was a lovely man and made sure we were looked after and given breakfast to eat in the morning. We were informed that some of the rebels were caught at night by the soldiers and that they were immediately executed and that their bodies were at the city centre. Some of us were intrigued and wanted to see if it was true so my cousin Abu, some other cousins and my siblings got into the car and drove to the centre, Abu had me on his back and we greeted the soldiers and we went over to where the dead bodies were. It was the first time I had ever seen a dead body and it was so gruesome. They had cut off the head of three of the rebels and placed their heads on sticks and their bodies lay on the floor, I think this was a clear message that the soldiers were not playing any games and were ready to protect the people of BO at any cost.

Soldiers and police were sent to our house to check that it was safe for us to return and as we returned immediately my father started making plans for us to return to Freetown but the only concern was that we had to travel by road and there was worry that there may be some rebels waiting along some of the highways and there may possibly be an attack on us. My father made some arrangements and we were given soldier escort to return back to Freetown and I can safely say that it was one of the most terrifying journeys of my life, I was too afraid to even take a nap at the possibility that I might wake up and find our car under attack. We returned to Freetown safely and after that things just didn't get back to normal, the government was trying really hard to keep the people safe while the rebels seemed to become more irritated as they started to slowly reach the capital from up country.

It wasn't long until my mother heard the news and on one faithful day I was outside playing with my friends and a young man came to our house with his ID and a message that he was sent by his Aunt who my mother had asked to take me back to England. I was totally shocked, unprepared and unaware and the first thought that came to my mind was my father. I wanted to see my father and he wasn't in the same city as me so I started to panic, I was told to quickly pack some things and while my cousin helped me pack and was talking about how I

was finally going to see my mother again I just
stood frozen just thinking about my father and
how much I would miss him and just when I
thought I had bonded with one parent I was
being rooted again and this time I felt deep
sorrow. I said my goodbyes to everyone at
home and one of my cousins escorted me and
the young man that was sent to come and
collect me and we went to my grandmother's
house for me to say my goodbyes. I won't lie
the entire time I was just wondering whether
or not I would get to speak to my father before
I left. We got to mama Hawa's house and she
was informed that I was being returned to my
mother in the UK, all my cousins started
hugging me and telling me goodbye and I tried
my best to fight the tears as my grandmother
held me and blessed me and by the time I knew
it we left and we were on our way to whoever
it was that would be taking me back to my
mother. As we sat in the taxi and drove past an
area I once hated, all the corners where me
and my cousins would play hide and seek tears
started to build up in my eyes because I
realised that the life I once desired so much to
leave behind I was now sad to leave. My family
lived in Kissy Dockyard in eastern Freetown,
an area which I had come to love so much and

as we drove into central town I sat in the car thinking about all the people I didn't get to say goodbye to and if I would ever see them again.

We got to this beautiful big house, I remember how beautiful it was and everything was mostly white and trendy. I waited in the lounge and this beautiful lady came over smiling and introduced herself to me, she said she was my mother's friend and she would be taking me back to see my mother and asked me if I was happy to see my mother again, I shook my head and said yes. I will call her Aunty V and that night I was given food to eat and given my own room to sleep and was told we were leaving early in the morning. Aunty V spent most of the night packing and preparing her bags until finally we all went to sleep. I was woken up very early in the morning around 5am to start getting ready and off we went after eating breakfast, on the way I recognised the area, we were back in Kissy at the Ferry dock were all the Ferry's going back and forth docked. It was so early and there were so many people, I remember seeing so many soldiers as the country was still under alert for the rebel war. There was a long line and we sat down for a few hours while documents were being checked and I realised that we were actually taking what looked like a cruise ship to sail to the Gambia and from there we would fly back to the UK because there was no flights leaving from Sierra Leone. As I sat there waiting for us to get onto the ship I kept hoping and wishing that I would see someone that I knew from home and wondered If somehow my father would find a way to make contact with me to say goodbye but that never happened. We finally got onto the ship and there were so many people and so many bags; hundreds of families trying to escape the war, I remember seeing so many young children on that ship and that gave me comfort because I knew I would have play mates because I heard that we would be on the ship for about three days. The ship started to sail and as we left the shores of Kissy Dockyard I could see my father's house from the ship and I wondered what my family were doing, if they missed me and for a moment I wanted to go back because for so long as much as I had dealt with so much pain I had become custom to it and this journey was another chapter that I was going into blindly and I didn't know what this one would entail.

The first night on the ship was okay, everyone seemed to be in good spirits and everyone seemed to be looking forward to what should have been a new beginning for everyone. There was sleeping areas made on the ship where families made their own beds with blankets and bed sheets and used their bags as pillows. We were given dinner and then breakfast on the first day, the kids played and the adults listened to music as the ship crew entertained us and kept us informed of our journey. There was a young girl my age that I played with everyday, she was with her parents and older siblings and her parents were nice and allowed me to sit with them during the day and even eat with them. I noticed very quickly that Aunty V seemed to become very aggravated when she was stressed or under pressure but she had this loud and joyful laugh. Aunty V also travelled with her daughter, her daughter's two children and another young girl who was a family friend's daughter who played with me and my new friend. On our final day on the ship everyone was excited and in good spirits we were on the coat of Gambia and the sun was shining so brightly and suddenly the ship stopped and everyone wondered what was

going on, the captain announced that there was
an malfunction which they needed to fix in
order for us to make the rest of the journey
and that we shouldn't panic. Hours went by and
we waited and waited and nothing happened,
the crew gave us food to eat and water to drink
and night time came and we slept the ship
didn't move.

The next day we were told that they couldn't
fix the problem and needed to call for aid from
the Gambian authorities that would need to
come and rescue us from the ship, I was
guessing that it would be a few hours and we
would be off the ship and on dry land but
rather than a few hours we were on the ship
for another three days. Something went wrong
and for some reason the Gambian authorities
delayed our rescue and we didn't know why,
the food that the crew was serving us had
finished because I am guessing that they only
catered for three days and had no emergency
supplies that could feed everyone on the ship
so families had to fend for themselves and
most families had brought supplies of food. The
first day we managed to get food from a friend
of Aunty V's for breakfast and lunch but
nothing for dinner, I managed to eat dinner

with my friend's family that evening. The second day in the morning my stomach started to rumble and I went to Aunty V and told her that I was really hungry and she yelled at me and stated that she didn't have any food and what did I expect her to do. I walked away because I was so ashamed because she screamed at me in the presence of other people. I sat the entire day with no food, I watched other families feeding their children with their supplies of biscuits and juice and some with corn flakes and dried milk, I watched and I cried because I had never in my life felt so hungry that I felt physically sick. By dinner time My friend's mother saw me in the corner crying and asked me what was wrong and I told her that I was really hungry and she asked me where my Aunty was I told her that she was on the other side of the ship but she said she didn't have any food. My friend's mother took my hand and took me over to where her family was and put me down with her kids and dished me some food from a container and gave me to eat while she explained to her family why I was crying and they moaned about how important it was for people to be aware of who they left in care of their children, I knew those comments were directed at Aunty V.

I went back to where Aunty V was and slept the night and the next day it was the same, I realised that Aunty V, her daughter and grand children had food to eat which they tried to eat discretely but there was none for me or the young girl that was also in their care. I spent that day crying again, my stomach hurt so bad that I started feeling dizzy and felt the need to vomit with nothing in my stomach to vomit out the cramps got worse. At one point I was in so much pain I couldn't walk and I collapsed just by ships kitchen as I silently cried for a few hours and during that time one of the kitchen staff came over to me and asked me what was wrong and I told him that I was hungry and haven't eaten all day, he stared at me with amazement and asked me where my family was and I explained to him just as I had done yesterday, he went into the kitchen and then came back and told me to go and sit under the stairs and he brought me a plate of food and some water and told me to eat but asked me to not make anyone see me. I realised that there was food on the ship but there wasn't enough for everyone so the food they had they used to feed their crew and sell food to the families who could buy or give to those who they knew. That guy helped me a lot; he gave me an element of trust, there was something about him that reminded me of my cousin Abu, he was so nurturing and kind. On the third day we were told that aid was on its way and within a few hours the British Red Cross sent lots of boats to offload families from the ship, I believe that the issue that the Gambian authorities had was immigration related and the Red Cross being a charity came to our rescue. While we were on the rescue boats their staff logged information on families and during that time some families stated that they hadn't made plans for housing but desperately had to leave Sierra Leone because of the pending war and what seemed like a new beginning for many was only a temporary plaster on a bleeding wound.

We arrived in Gambia and we were taken to a friend of Aunty V's who had a big house in central Gambia. For some reason we were undercover almost as though we were not suppose to be staying in the house. I gathered that the house did not belong to Aunty V's friend. We spent what seemed like two weeks in a dark and over crowded room day and night not being able to go outside and play or even have any fresh air. Aunty V found a place for us to stay and we moved into a two bedroom apartment which was in a compound shared with about six other families, with all the apartments side to side and facing each other, it wasn't the richest of areas but to me it was better than being locked in a dark room for weeks at a time. I was so happy when we moved to this house because it was a space of our own while we waited for documents to be prepared for me to return back to my mother was what I told. The wait became longer and longer and it just seemed as though it was a repeat of living in Sierra Leone with my father wishing and hoping that my mother would send for me to return to her. There was a huge difference living with my family in Sierra Leone and living with total strangers because in Sierra Leone no matter what I encountered I had at least one person that was fighting for me but in the hands of Aunty V's family it started to become a story of slavery, imprisonment and sorrow. Aunty V had her own room, her daughter and her kids had their own room and me and the other girl Jeneba that they were looking after slept on the floor in the lounge, we didn't complain because as bad as things would get it felt like me and Jeneba only had each other and needed to stick together. Things got from bad to worse in the house; me and Jeneba became the house girls for Aunty V, her daughter and her grandchildren. We did all the cleaning, laundry and helped to cook and wash the pots and pans after everyone finished eating. Aunty V made it so clear to us that we were not her family because we saw the difference of how she treated her daughter and her grandchildren and how she treated us.

Some days when Aunty V's daughter would cook she would give a portion of food that was so small that we wouldn't be full, on some days we wouldn't even have breakfast but she would make sure that she called her children into the bedroom close the door and gave them food to eat. They would come out of the room smelling of sardine and their empty cups which would have the evidence of tea in them. I wondered so many times how someone could be so cruel to other people's children; I then started blaming our parents that entrusted us in the hands of people who just didn't have a heart to care for children that they did not birth. Me and Jeneba became so close to our next door

neighbor who had younger children our age
and a teenage daughter who was fond of me
and Jeneba but was especially fond of me
because of the great stories I would tell her
about Sierra Leone and my dad who she loved
to hear me speak about. Our neighbors quickly
noticed what was happening in the house on
the basis of how Aunty V and her daughter and
children treated us and spoke to us, we
confided in the neighbors daughter and
whenever Aunty V and her daughter and
children would go out and me and Jeneba were
left at the house alone we would spend those
hours playing freely like children who were
free and loved and cared for. Our neighbors
daughter would sneak and give us food to eat
on the days when we didn't have enough or
didn't eat breakfast, she would call us over to
pretend that we were helping her with
something and she would give us bread and
cheese to eat and some tea or mixed cool-aid.
A time came when we became so hungry that
we started stealing some of the raw rice in the
house that Aunty V's daughter kept and we
would soak the rice with water and sugar in a
bowl for an hour and once the rice was a little
soft we would go to the back off the house with
two spoons and me and Jeneba would hide and

eat it. We did this for a little while without being caught until one day when one of Aunty V's grandchildren found our hiding place where we hid our stash of soaked rice and they went and told their mother and let's just say we were shamed and beaten and the rice was moved from the lounge into her bedroom. The weeks pasted and the treatment just got worst, we normally took our shower in the evening when we were done with our work. We would bail water and shower together and everyday as I was bathing I would cry bitterly and ask God to please send someone to rescue us, Jeneba was so strong because she would only cry because she didn't want to see me cry, she would place her hand on my face and start wiping my tears away and tell me "FA don't cry, I know that your mum is going to come for you soon please don't cry ". Jeneba was a different type of strong, she had adapted to the abuse that she accepted that this was just a part of her story whereas I found it so difficult that this was my story and I refused to emotionally accept that this would be my life.

There was a day when my neighbor was going to buy something for her mother and she

wanted me to come with her, I told her that I
would really love to go with her because we
never get to go out and pleaded with her to
find a way to get her mother to speak to Aunty
V to allow me to go with her and indeed on that
day God spoke because Aunty V agreed for me
to accompany this young girl on her errand and
we left the house. I was in such a good mood, I
smiled as I watched people walk past and to
see the real power of the sun and how it shined
bright in the sky, I watched the school children
walk by playing and running and I wished that
was me but I was just glad to be out of that
house if only for a little while. On the way back
to the house we walked past a man who
shouted " Fatmata, Fatmata Bockari " and I
was shocked because I didn't know him and I
was in a country where I had no family or
friends. The man walked closer to me and my
neighbors daughter and said " Fatmata,
daughter of Solokor and Zainab " and straight
away my heart started beating really fast and I
was confused and in that moment as this man
looked me from head to toe in total shock my
neighbors daughter stepped in and asked the
man if he knew me and the man went on to
explain that he knew my parents very well and
that he is so appalled to see me in such a state

and asked to know what was going on. My neighbors daughter started to explain everything I was being subjected to in the house and begged this man to make contact with my mother and tell her the truth of what I was really going through, the man looked me in the eye and asked me "Fatmata is this true "I bowed my head down first and once I looked back up at him I just exploded and burst into tears and started crying bitterly and he grabbed me into a hug and comforted me. He promised me that he would contact my mother and tell her everything we have told him and told me to be patient. He thanked my neighbor's daughter and blessed her and also gave her some money and told her to use it to buy food for me and Jeneba whenever we didn't eat. The man left us and walked away and I hugged my older friend and thanked her for being there for me and she smiled and hugged me back and told me "You see, I told that one day God would sort this all out ", we stopped and got some food to eat before we returned home and also bought some food for Jeneba.

What seemed like 2-3 weeks passed and one day as we sat down outside the apartment two

people came and introduced themselves to
Aunty V and her daughter and stated that they
were sent by my mother, they called whoever
sent them and gave the phone to Aunty V and
me and Jeneba looked on in shock. Aunty V
gave the phone back and she seemed to be in
shock herself and looked over to me and said "
Fatmata your leaving, you're going to stay with
your mother's friend, go inside and pack your
things". My heart was beating so fast and I
almost felt as though I couldn't breathe, I
grabbed Jeneba's hand and pulled her along
with me as we went into the apartment and into
Aunty V's daughter's bedroom where our
clothes were. I turned back and looked at
Jeneba and burst into tears and she hugged me
and also started crying, we cried together and
she kept telling me "I told you Fatmata, I told
you that your mum would come for you ". I
didn't realise that as much as I prayed for this
day I didn't expect that I would feel so much
sorrow; my heart was heavy and I didn't have
much time to say goodbye. I cried as I packed
the little belongings I had and Jeneba told me
to stop crying and I told her "I can't leave you,
I don't want to leave you, you won't have
anyone, I can't leave you here ". We hugged
and cried even more and Jeneba told me that

she was going to be okay and I shouldn't worry
and I made a promise to her that I would come
back for her soon. I told her that I would tell
my mum about her and we would come back
for her, I promised Jeneba that I would never
forget her and everyday at the same time that
we prayed while we showered wherever I was
I would be praying for her and she smiled and
cried and gave me her last hug. I said a teary
goodbye to everyone in the compound and
walked away with the people that came to
collect me and when I reached the end
entrance of the compound I turned back just to
see Jeneba's face one last time and she was
stood in a corner where no one would see her
and she cried as she waved to me and I cried
as they took me away. That was the end of me
and Jeneba's chapter but a day didn't pass
when I didn't think about her, sometimes I sit
down and imagine where she is now, is she
married, does she have children; is she happy.
Some days I pray that God would find a way to
reconnect us just so I could tell her that I was
sorry that life didn't permit me to go back for
her and to really thank her for being my
guardian angel at a time when I had nobody, I
hold Jeneba in my spirit and I pray that the
bitterness of her ordeals didn't wash away all

the goodness in her soul.

I arrived to what was a rich family home on the other side of town where all the rich ministers, ambassadors and business tycoons lived. This house was nice, everything was bright and clean and I was welcomed by Aunty A who was my mother's friend. Aunty A lived with her husband, three children, one who was four or five years older than me and her name was Isi and a daughter who was exactly my age called Ram. Aunty A also had her older sister living with her who also had an adult daughter who would have been at least 21 years old at the time. Aunty A's youngest daughter had Down syndrome and severs learning disabilities. They had two maids and a driver and also Aunty A's husband's younger brother living in their care. It was a relief to move in with them, I shared a room with Aunty A's daughter who was the same age as me "Ram", Ram was a spoilt daddy's girl who seemed to get her way with her parents whenever she felt like it. Aunty A's husband was a political minister who was under investigation for some type of government fraud and the families properties were seized and they were forced to downsize and live just

a little bit richer than before but to be fair I
didn't see much of a difference. My mother
called me and we spoke and she explained to
me that she heard what was happening with
Aunty V and was so sorry for what I had to go
through and promised me that I wouldn't stay
with Aunty A for too long as she was in the
process of trying to get me back to the UK but
there were some issues that she was trying to
deal with. I told my mother that I wanted to go
to school and I didn't want to stay home and
she told me that she had already spoken to
Aunty A about that and they were in the
process of trying to get me into the same
school as Aunty A's daughter Ram who was
attending a well respected private school.

The first month with Aunty A was amazing, I
was eating as I was suppose to and playing just
like children my age did. I loved the area
where Aunty A and her family lived, it was a
rich neighborhood and every house you passed
there lived a minister of foreign ambassador.
The neighborhood was beautiful with trees and
flowers that made the sun seem much more
appealing. This neighborhood wasn't the type
of place where you saw people hanging around
outside or children screaming, it was the type

of neighborhood where every morning you saw
the jeeps and Land rovers driving outside of
the gated houses and in the evening you would
see the same. It was quiet and peaceful and
every day we heard the sounds of the birds
that sat peacefully in the trees. It seemed like
five months passed and still I wasn't attending
school but I was home every day while I
watched Aunty A's two daughters go to school
every morning, the driver would drop them at
school and also pick them up. At this time I
was no longer living in luxury, I wasn't being
treated the same as Aunty A's children
anymore like I did when I first started living
with them; I don't know what changed but I
know that I felt like it was just like living with
Aunty V all over again the only difference was
that I was living in a nice atmosphere. Every
morning my job would be to wake up and
sweep the entire house and wipe down the
floors. I would also have to do the same in
Aunty A's room and her sister's room. Aunty
A's sister wasn't a very nice person, she would
make me wipe her falls down twice to make
sure that it was spotless and if it wasn't done
to her satisfaction she would ask me to do it
again. Some days I would be so tired from all
the work that I would voice out to her that I

was tired and she would tell me to shut up and just wipe her floors, at one point she even got a cane and would sit on her bed with her cane while she watched me on my knees wiping her floors. They had two maids in the house, one that cooked and the other that looked after their youngest daughter who had learning disabilities; for some reason I became their daughters part time nanny, it was my responsibility to feed her every morning and keep her entertained throughout the day until everyone else was back home.

There was a family that lived across the road in a gated unfinished land; the family lived in a metal built one room (Panbody) as it is referred to in Sierra Leone. This was a family of mother and father and four of their children, they lived poor with very limited resources. The father was a brick layer and only worked as and when he was accepted on building sites and that is how he supported his family. The mother sold little cooking items at the local market as and when she had the resources and none of their children attended school because they couldn't afford school fees. I first met the family when I first moved to Aunty A's house, one night after everyone had finished eating Aunty A's husband's younger brother Mo who I was very fond off asked me to follow him to dispose of the leftovers. I followed Mo to the back of the house and watched him scrape all of the leftover food from everyone's plates into one large bowl and covered it and told me to follow him. We left the house and walked across the street to where this family lived and as we entered the gated walls I was shocked to see that level of poverty in an area that was so rich but I was amazed to also witness peace and happiness in those gated walls. The children played and danced and chased each other around and I smiled because that was the first time I realised that money was not the root of all happiness. MO greeted the family and introduced me as the new addition to his family and I smiled and waved to them, the family had all daughters and one of them was near in age to me and she was the one who took the bowl from MO as the parents thanked MO. MO signaled for us to leave and as I was walking away I stopped and looked back at the family and saw them all gathered around the bowl happily eating the leftovers we had given them and that to me was humility at a level that I had never experienced before. We went back to the house and that night as I lay down to sleep I

was so thankful because for the first time I had
seen people who seemed like they had so much
to cry and be sad about but they chose to be
happy and in that moment I decided to accept
my life for what it was and just live in the
moment until God was ready to save me from
what seemed to be another horrific chapter in
my life.

A few more weeks went by and there I was
settled in my role as the part time cleaner and
nanny doing as I was told everyday just so that
peace could reign. In the evenings it was my
job to empty the leftovers and take it over to
the family, I used this time to bond with their
eldest daughter Hajah who became my close
friend, me and Hajah would spend our
afternoons playing in her compound while we
both tried to forget that we couldn't attend
school. Hajah's story was different because her
family couldn't afford to pay her school fees;
my story was because my carer was cruel. My
mother's phone calls started to feel like guilt
trips to me, she always sounded so happy and
seemed like she had so much trust and faith in
her friend Aunty A that I didn't want to sound
like the child that is always being mistreated. I
started to think that maybe it was me, maybe

there was something wrong with me, maybe
my father's family didn't have a choice but to
love and accept me but these strangers didn't
have to, maybe that was why I was being
mistreated; I was an unlovable child that was
why it was so easy for my parents to pass me
around like a volleyball. Aunty A would always
be sitting right next to me while I spoke to my
mother, it was almost comic to see how the
abuser knows that they are abusing the power
that they have been given but still they are
never willing to change.

One afternoon as I sat alone outside the house
with nothing to do than to listen to the sound of
the birds and watch the planes go by in the sky
a little girl approached me. She was dark
skinned like Lupita and she had the long
braided hair and a beautiful smile that warmed
my heart, her black skin was so beautiful, she
came and sat right next to me and smiled with
her perfect white teeth on display and said " Hi
what's your name ", I told her I was called
Fatmata and asked her what her name was and
she told me her name was Adama. Adama
asked me why I wasn't in school like everyone
else and I told her that I was still waiting to
start school and asked her why she wasn't in

school and she told me that she hasn't been feeling well for a few days so her parents kept her home from school. Adama was seven years old and told me that she lived with her parents and her older brother Jeffery. Both of Adama's parents worked for the United Nations and they lived very well in one of the nicest houses in the neighborhood. Adama asked me about my life and I told a little bit about living in the UK and living in Sierra Leone and explained to her that I was waiting for my mother to come and get me and take me back. Adama spoke so well and was very intelligent; she sat with me for over an hour as we talked as kids did about our favorite food and TV shows. After that day Adama became so attached to me, she would come by and see me outside the house every other day after she came home from school. I spent my mornings doing house work and the rest of the day I would go over to Hajah's house and we would play together. One day Aunty A called me into her room and told me that she had been informed that I was spending the afternoon over at Hajah's house and asked me why I was going there and I told Aunty A that I go there to play with Hajah because I get bored at the house and no one in the house allows me to watch TV during the day. Aunty A told me that if I was bored I could spend my time looking after the baby at home and she warned to stop going over to that family's house and asked me if I didn't know the type of friends to make. I was so sad, my heart fell down in my chest because Hajah and her family had become a great distraction for me, they kept me entertained everyday and took me apart of their family and Aunty A told me that I couldn't associate with them anymore because they were poor, this was heartbreaking.

I did as I was told and limited my time with Hajah's family, I would still see Adama some days after she came home from school but it wasn't the same as me and Hajah. Me and Aunty A's daughter Ram clashed a lot, Ram was very spoilt and had this heavy spirit of jealousy, she reminded me so much of my step sister in Sierra Leone. Ram seemed to have everything she wanted, her mother spoiled her rotten and they treated her as though as she was an only child. Aunty A would travel to the UK sometimes and I would be so excited because I knew on her return my mother would send me lots of goodies, the first time she went she returned with two suitcases of clothes for

Ram and took out 3 dresses and gave me to me
and said it was from my mother, this happened
a few times and every time I would happily
take those clothes and keep them as going out
garments. I could count the amount of clothes
that I had, they wouldn't fill a plastic bag.
Sometimes when Ram was tired with her old
clothes she would give them to me and I was
happy to accept because it meant that I had
something other than my five garments of
clothes that I would hand wash and wear
weekly. I always wondered why my mother
would only send me three or four clothes
whenever Aunty A would go to London, I
didn't even have decent shoes to go out with, I
wore slippers whenever I went out if the family
decided that they would take me along with
them. I struggled at the hands of this family,
things just seemed to get worse for me and I
couldn't understand what I was doing wrong.
Aunty A painted a different picture about whom
I was to everyone around her, she refused to
tell people who I was, she didn't even tell
anyone that I was her friend's daughter but
instead she labeled me as a refugee from
Sierra Leone that her family was trying to help.
I would get so angry when she said that
because it felt as though she was wiping away

my identity, she was trying to belittle me and take anyway my right to be Fatmata Bockari the daughter of Zainab and Solokor, I didn't want to be Fatmata the abandoned refugee as her family labeled me; A time came when I just accepted the label and stopped trying to tell my story when people would ask me.

Something good must have happened because one day my mother called and told me that I would be starting school, she said that she had spoken to Aunty A and she would make arrangements for me to attend the same school as Ram. I was so happy, I thanked my mother and on that day it felt like everything that was happening in that house didn't matter to me anymore because I was about to start school. I couldn't wait, my mum told me that Aunty A would take me shopping for my school uniform, school bags and shoes. Me and Aunty A left the house a few days later to go shopping, I was so happy and it felt like all my dreams had come true. We went to a local market and as we went through Aunty A shopped for herself buying herself lace material and things she needed to cook and after forty minutes of shopping for herself she took me over to a used shoe stall to buy some school shoes. It was a used shoes stall where you would be lucky to find a size that fit you. Aunty A asked the seller to help me find my size, I was a size four then and we went through all of the girls shoes there and there was no size fours only threes. Aunty A asked me to try on the size three which I did and I told her that it was tight and Aunty A told me that I would have to manage the size three because they didn't have my size, we bought the shoes and left. Aunty A took me to what I thought was Ram's private school to register me , we drove to the school and with pride I smiled and watched as we drove straight past Ram's school and parked right outside a public school that was two minutes away. This was a school that the poorest of the poorest families attended and as we got out of the car I was in total shock because I didn't understand what was going on, we walked into the school and I noticed that most of the children wore slippers instead of shoes and at that moment tears started to form in my eyes but I fought so hard to not allow them to fall. I didn't have a choice and at this point I was registered and was scheduled to start the following Monday. On the way home in the car I just sat back and thought about how openly wicked Aunty A was being to me, At this point I started to realise that I was being maltreated. Aunty A told me that although my mother had informed me that I would be going to the same school as Ram that wouldn't be possible because school fees need to be paid and my mother hasn't sent the money and her and her husband cannot afford to pay my school fees because they have their two children's fees to consider. She told me that when I speak to my mother I should never tell her that I am not attending Ram's school because she would feel bad, I agreed and that evening when my mother called I did as Aunty A stated and told her I had been enrolled in Ram's school and would be starting on Monday.

My schooling was another horrific journey that left a bitter taste in my mouth and scars on my body. I used Ram's used school bag and socks when I started school and for the first few days I rode with Ram and Isis to school, the driver would drop us all off at their school and I would walk down the road to my school. By the following week Aunty A and her sister both told me that I am missing my chores at home and needed to wake up earlier to do all the cleaning and feed the baby and then take a taxi to school. I didn't understand because this so called baby was actually four years old and already had her nanny so it just started to feel as though they just wanted to oppress me. I didn't have a choice so I started doing as I was told, school started at 9am so I would wake up at 6am every morning to make sure I sweep and mop the entire house, feed the baby, eat breakfast, have a wash and get dressed in time to leave the house and make my way to school. The money that they gave me was only enough for one thing, either I used it for transportation to school or I used it as lunch money to buy food. Ram and Isi had packed lunches prepared for them every day by the maid but I was given transport fare that they knew would not be enough for my travels and for my lunch. Every morning I had to make the decision on whether I would eat at school and walk one hour and a half to school and one hour and a half back home and every day I had to make the decision to eat at school. I would fill up my water bottle with water to keep me hydrated on the walk back home from school because the heat was at its highest then, the mornings were not so bad but the afternoons were bad.

I use to walk so much that some days I would

stop alongside the and just to cry because I
was so tired and these were on the days when
I didn't have money to buy food at school or
pay for a taxi to school so I would be under
that hot sun walking in shoes that were one
size too small for me, with a hungry stomach
and weak legs. Some days I would be so
hungry in school from the walking and lack of
food that I would sleep during class and the
teacher would beat me. This is normal in
African public schools, it's not seen as abuse
but rather discipline. Most days on my way
home I would be praying to God as I cried and I
would plead with God to help me out of the hell
pit that I was in, some days I would just pray
that I could find money on the floor, I prayed
for the weirdest things and most days God
would answer my prayer on the days that I
didn't have money for food some of my friends
at school would share their food with me. The
food that was sold at this school was street
food, it was the street sellers that would come
to the school gates at lunch time and sell to the
children. Walking home became so unbearable
because my shoes were so tight, I was 10
years old and developed corns on my toes
because of this, I started packing my flip flops
in my school bag and once I left the house I

would wear them to walk to school and walk back home. Once I got home every day I would soak my feet in cold water because they burned so badly. Although it was clear to me that I was being mistreated I was just grateful that I could go to school and be around other children for a few hours a day, this made me feel normal in a sense because I didn't have to think about my life back at the house. The school I attended was a Muslim school so it was compulsory that I took Quran classes, I was proud because this was something that my grandmother mama hawa desired for me to do, I promised myself that I would learn as much as I could and once I got back to the UK I would call my grandmother and surprise her by reading the Quran to her; unfortunately I was only able to learn the very first part which is the first prayer.

Time went on and my stay in Gambia became very unbearable, I was already being physically, emotionally and mentally abused but the physical abuse went a step further at the hands of Aunty A's daughter Ram and her cousins. One weekend the family had gone out and left me at home with the maids and as always I would either sneak to go and play with

Hajah but on this day I just decided to sit down
outside the house and listen to the birds sing.
Along came beautiful and joyful Adama who
was always excited to ask me about how
school was for me and today I just wasn't in
the mood to lie so I poured my heart out to
Adama and expressed that I really missed my
mother and that I wasn't happy. Adama put her
arms around me and told me that she didn't like
to see me sad and that she missed my smile as
she chuckled and lay her head on my shoulder,
that was such a great source of comfort for me
and exactly what I needed at that time. Adama
told me that since I was home alone I should
come over to her house so we could play but I
was skeptical, Adama told me not to worry that
I would be back before Aunty A and her family
returned which would be a few hours since
they had gone to Banjul. I agreed and followed
Adama to her house, we walked and talked as
we strolled across the road to her gated house
which was painted in black and white and had
high walls I was so amazed when I entered to
what seemed to be a hidden palace behind
those high walls. I stood in astonishment as
Adama laughed and pulled me along as we
passed the two expensive parked cars in their
big drive way. We entered Adama's lounge and

yet again I was blown away, this family was truly living in luxury; the fifty inch television was a testament of that. A few moments later a calm and nurturing voice called for Adama and soon enough we saw the face of this beautiful chocolate skinned woman with the whitest teeth and the most beautiful smile, Adam definitely looked like her mother. Adama's mother was tall and slim and took very good care of herself. she had a weave on but not the type that made her look like a social experiment but the type that just enhanced her beauty, Adama's mother walked over to me with a big smile and introduced herself to me as Adama's mother and told me that Adama had told her so much about me and that she was very happy to finally meet me, I was so nervous but this woman reminded me so much of mother, she was so nurturing; she was like a mother earth, I could feel so much love and positive energy.

We were given some snacks and juice to eat as we sat and watched some TV in the lounge and a few moments later Adama's older brother Jeffrey who was exactly the same age as me walked into the house looking like a young NBA player. I know I was young but I know

fine when I see it and Jeffery was international
fine, he was tallish, with perfect long legs and
a black America model type of face; he looked
like a younger version of Denzel Washington
with a baby face. Adama introduced us and
Jeffery stared at me with such depth it felt like
he was looking into my soul and I felt
something that I had never felt before, my
heart was beating really fast and I felt like I
started to sweat. I think Jeffery was the first
boy I liked and I hated that thump in my heart
so I looked down at the empty cup that I was
still pretending to sip from as Jeffery walked to
his room spinning the basket ball on his
fingers. Adama told me to go to her room to
play and as you would expect Adama had all
the latest toys, baby dolls and even a computer
in her room that we played on for so long; it
felt so refreshing to just forget my life with
Aunty A and just be a child again even if it was
just for a few hours. Adama's mother called us
into the dining room and as we entered Jeffery
was already sitting at the dinner table that was
already set with plates of food that glazed with
chicken and spaghetti that was my favorite. Me
and Adama joined Jeffery at the table and her
mother came over to me and pushed my chair
in properly and placed a napkin on my lap and

poured some juice in my glass before doing the same for Adama, it doesn't seem like much but that little moment of care meant so much to me; It was so easy to forget what it felt like to be cared for, it was easy to forget that I was actually still a child that still needed care and nurturing. Adama's mother asked me questions about my family and where I was from, I think Adama had already explained to her mother what I was going through because she had the deepest look of guilt and sorrow in her eyes, only a mother would understand that feeling; to look at another woman's child being mistreated and there isn't much you can do but she didn't realise that the love she showed me that day gave me so much hope of me being reunited with my mother.

The months passed and things became more extreme, Jeffery and Adama grew fonder of me and that started causing more issues me. Jeffery would send Adama to come and call me to come outside and we would all just sit and laugh at Adama's comic behavior. I would always invite Ram to come and sit with us because I realised that she had a huge crush on Jeffery and Aunty A did everything possible to try and befriend Adama's mother but for some reason unknown to me she refused Aunty A's friendship. One weekend I was in the back of the house washing clothes and Aunty A called me to the lounge where her, her daughters, her niece and her sister were all sitting and she told me that Adama's mother had sent some sweets and chocolates over for me, she also told me that she was aware that I had been going over to their house and asked me if I told Adama's mother anything and I told her no. Ram sat down right next to her mother adding insults and claiming that I was forcing a friendship with Adama and Jeffery and I was making the family look bad because why would Jeffery's mother send gifts for me and not her and her sister. Aunty A refused to give me the sweets and chocolates and told me off so badly that I cried she told me that I was no longer given the permission to leave the house without telling anyone and neither was I to go to their house again.

It felt like my life was falling apart and every time that I prayed for God to send me some happiness they did everything possible to take it away. I don't know what happened that Ram became extremely jealous of me over the next few weeks she would tell lies on me just so I would get in trouble with her mother and get beaten. It felt like I was walking on egg shells most of the time, one weekend Ram's cousins came over to spend the weekend and they all ganged up on me that night and took all the bed sheets and covers so I would have to sleep on an empty sponge on the floor. I didn't complain I just ignored all of their comments as they mocked me and laughed at me and threw their shoes at my head, I remained calm because I knew they were trying to push me so they would have a reason to either get me in trouble or have a reason to attack me so I just closed my eyes and went to sleep. It was the shock at woke me up and the cold and the wetness, Ram and her cousin threw an entire bucket of water over me while I was asleep, I instantly burst into tears because I didn't understand what I had done wrong so I got up from the soaked foam and realised that it was morning. They stood watching me as they laughed and called me names, as I went towards the door two of them blocked me and said I wasn't going anywhere until I vowed to stop forcing people to like it me. I forced my hand against the door to open it and that's when they all jumped on me and started hitting me and pulling my hair, I did my best to fight them off but they just

continued so I became so enraged that and
suddenly strength came and I just went into
beast mode, I threw Ram on one side of the
room and kicked her cousins so badly that they
all screamed and fell and that's when I opened
the door and started running; I didn't know
where I was going but I ran and left the house
and ran straight to Hajah's house in flood of
tears, Hajah's parents consoled me and gave
me some dry clothes to wear.

I spent the entire day with Hajah, we actually
didn't stay at her house because we knew Ram
and her cousins or her mother would send for
them to come and look for me so we went to
one of our local play areas and spent the day
lost in an imaginary world. I was so afraid to go
back to the house that I didn't return until 8pm
at night. I had spent the entire day away from
the house without them knowing where I was
and most importantly for them I hadn't
performed my maid duties especially when it's
the weekend when the maids were off duty.
Aunty A didn't care that her daughter and
nieces attacked me, all that mattered to her
was that she had to get out of her bed earlier
than she normally does to feed and wash her
own child. I was flogged badly that day but

because I was expecting it I guess it wasn't as painful when it actually happened. Ram and her cousins continued in their bid to make my life uncomfortable, her cousins started visiting every other weekend just so they could fight with me; it actually became a routine. One weekend we all travelled to Banjul and during that stay they set me up to me attacked at the local market by a young girl whose boyfriend had taken a liking to me, that girl attacked me in the middle the street with the help of Ram and her cousins, I went back to the house with a bruised arm and a bloody lip and none of the adults did or said anything about it. A point came when I just wanted to end my life because it started to feel as though no one wanted me, my parents didn't care about me enough that's why I was in that situation and those who are suppose to be taking care of me kept abusing me, none of this made sense to me.

A few months down the line my mother called and informed us that my sister Rakie would be coming to visit me in Gambia, I was so excited but Aunty A and her family were not so happy. They started acting really nice the week that Rakie was suppose to arrive, they told me that

while my sister was around I didn't have to do
any of the house work because I would need
time to spend with her. Aunty A also gave me a
few of Ram's clothes to wear while my sister
was in town, they took me to the hair salon and
had my hair done properly to ensure that I
looked like a child that was being looked after.
Rakie arrived and as my sister is in nature she
came with gifts for everyone and lots of
presents and clothes for me which made me so
happy. While my sister was there she called
my mum everyday and we spoke and that made
me feel loved. Aunty A was always on edge,
she made sure that whenever me and Rakie
wanted to go somewhere she would send
either Ram or her niece Nancy to go along with
us and Rakie quickly picked up on this. So one
evening she pulled me to a corner to told me
that we would be leaving very early in the
morning and told me not to say anything to
anyone but to ensure that I was washed and
dressed by 9am, I agreed and did as my sister
instructed. The next morning we were the first
up, washed and dressed and ate breakfast
early, by the time Aunty A and the rest of them
got up we were about to leave the house.
Aunty A had this look of horror on her face
when she realised that we would be leaving

without one of them following us, she told my
sister to wait a little while for Ram or her niece
to bath and get ready to escort us and Rakie
informed Aunty A not to worry because a
friend of hers in Gambia has sent her driver to
pick us up down the road and we need to rush
to meet him. The expression on all of their
faces was priceless, it was like when someone
had swallowed poison and was just waiting to
die. Me and my sister left the house and
laughed when we got outside because we were
able to dodge their monitoring for a day. My
sister took me to get some ice cream and as
we sat and I ate she told me that the real
reason she was here was because her and mum
had a feeling that I wasn't happy or being
treated fairly and when she arrived she noticed
a few things and also noticed that Aunty A
always wanted someone to follow us when she
wants to take me out and that made her
suspect that they didn't want her to be alone
with me. Rakie told me to tell her the truth and
tell her absolutely everything, and off course I
didn't hold back I told her everything, about my
schooling, the abuse at the house, my lack of
clothes and the far distances I have to walk
every day.

Rakie burst into tears and kept telling me that she knew that they were mistreating me, she went on to tell me that my mum sends two suitcases of clothes and shoes for me whenever Aunty A is coming back to Gambia from Manchester, which meant that Aunty A was actually giving her daughter all the things that my mother and sister were sending for me. I started crying when my sister started telling me about everything that my mother had been doing for me, all the money she sends and she was so angry to learn that I wasn't even in a private school since that's what my mother had been paying for. As we sat there Rakie called my mother and explained everything to her, Rakie was crying as she was talking to my mum and she handed the phone over to me to speak to her; when I took the phone my mother asked me if everything that Rakie had said was true and I told her yes and she burst into tears and told me that she was so sorry that I had to go through this again and promised me that she is coming very soon to come and take me. She begged me to be patient and try my best to not get into trouble, my mother and sister spoke and from what I later understood was that the delay was due to my passport being lost but after that phone call things seemed to speed up. The rest of Rakie's stay was great, I loved having my sister around because she was so fun and always made me laugh so the day that she left I cried like a baby because I knew that things were about to go back to normal. My sister gave me some money to hide away that I would be using to get a taxi to school instead of walking and buy myself lunch at school. Rakie left that evening and I spent the night crying until the next day when Aunty A's sister told me to go and change from the new clothes I was wearing that my sister had sent me and wear one of my old rags so I would get dirt on it while I was wiping her falls down. A month later I got a phone call from my mother and off course Aunty A was nearby to monitor the phone call, my mum informed me that she was going to tell me something and all I needed to do was listen to what she was telling me and say okay and not tell anyone. I agreed and my mother went on to tell me that she would be coming to get me in a week's time, I couldn't believe what I was hearing, my heart started beating really fast as my mother continued to give me the details of what time she would arrive and so on. I was in total shock, I had waited so long to hear those words from my mother and finally it happened. She told me to not say a word to anyone, she told me that she would be at the house by 5pm latest the following Wednesday, she also told me that she didn't want them to know that she was coming because she wanted to see exactly how they are caring for me. I put the phone down and Aunty A asked me what my mother said and I told her that she was just giving me messages from my sisters and brothers. The week couldn't have gone faster for me, I was so excited it almost felt as though I was walking on cloud 9; the funniest thing is that during this particular week everyone in the household was being extra horrible; I saw it all as a sign that I was indeed about to leave. Wednesday came and I couldn't sit still, I rushed to finish my house work and wanted to have enough time to go and sit outside and wait for my mum but that day everyone was out and it was just me, the maids and Aunty A's husband at home and he was not in a pleasant mood at all that day.

I can't remember exactly what I was doing but I know I was in such a hyper mood that Aunty A's husband called me into his study area and told me to sit down in the corner because I was disturbing him. I sat down on the tiled floor in my ragged top and skirt that I wanted to

change before my mother arrived. I asked
Aunty A's husband if I could go and get
changed because my clothes were wet from
doing the laundry and he refused and told me
to remain seated. There was a clock right
above where Aunty A's husband was sat and it
was 11:45am, My heart was beating really fast
because I was so nervous, I was praying in my
mind that everything would be fine with my
mother's journey and that she wouldn't get lost
on the way or that anything negative would
happen. My legs were numb from sitting for so
long, I looked at the clock again at it was
2.30pm, I asked Aunty A's husband if I could go
to the toilet and again he refused even after I
told him that I was desperate; So I sat down
with my legs squeezed together to stop the pee
from wanting to come out.

 I tried to take my mind away from the fact that
I needed to pee and started thinking about what
my mother looked like now and if she would be
happy to see me, and then I remember that
there was so many bad things that she would
have to find out, more than anything I was just
happy that she was coming. I tried really hard
to keep it in but I couldn't, I looked at the clock
again and it was 3.45pm and my bladder wasn't

that strong so I ended up wetting myself. My underwear and skirt was wet so I slowly moved away from the puddle of pee feeling ashamed and angry at myself for not holding my bladder together for longer. I sat as tears rolled down my face while I listened to the noise of the CNN news broadcasters coming from Aunty A's husband's radio. I looked at the clock again and it was finally time, it was 4.55pm and I stretched my hearing to listen to the cars go past the street, Aunty A's husbands radio was loud but my desire to see my mother exceeded so somehow I could hear everything happening outside. I looked at the clock again and it was 5.20pm and she still was here, cars drove by and each time my heart started beating as I would listen to hear if they stopped outside the house. I started wondering if something had happened, what if she didn't get on her flight or if she is lost in Gambia, I was so restless. I heard the sound of a car that was very loud and it was loud because it stopped right out the house, the car engine was still on and the car stood outside for a few minutes as I listened and I heard the car door slam the car drove away and a few moments later there was a ring at the door and my heart started beating really fast again, I didn't want to get excited in case it

wasn't her but I couldn't help it. One of the
maids walked past the corridor where I was sat
and went and opened the door and straight
away I heard her say " Hi, I am Zainab, I am
Fatmata's mother " at that moment I didn't care
because there was nothing they could do to
hurt me anymore so I jumped up and ran as
Aunty A's husband shouted for me to come
back, I ran into the toilet and took my wet
panties off and ran straight down the corridor
as the maid was shouting for me I appeared
and there she was; I ran and jumped into my
mother's arms, I hugged her so tightly that she
couldn't move. She smelt so good, she was
wearing the Eternity perfume by Calvin Klein
which was her favorite;. My mother pulled my
head away from her shoulders and said "let me
look at you properly my baby ", she started
crying and told me how much she missed me
and started rubbing my body and felt that my
skirt was wet and asked me what happened, I
instantly put my head down and in that moment
Aunty A's husband, the other maids and Aunty
A's sister all gathered in shock. My mother
greeted them all but they were all speechless
but tried their best to welcome her and offered
her a seat in the lounge. My mother went and
sat in the lounge with me on her lap as she

continued to shed tears and kept looking at my undone hair and the dirty clothes I was wearing. Aunty A's sister entertained my mother until Aunty A returned home, she looked like someone who had been caught stealing. She ran and hugged my mother and greeted her and told her how shocked she was to see her and asked my mother why she didn't tell them she was coming, my mother told Aunty A that it was actually a last minute arrangement because immigration contacted her regarding my lost passport and told her she needed to come here to make some arrangements for my travel. Aunty A wasn't convinced but they all sat down with the look of shame on all of their faces with no explanation and too ashamed to say anything so my mother told Aunty A that she would take me to the hotel with her tonight because we had an early appointment at the British embassy in the morning. My mother told Aunty A that we would be back tomorrow or the day after once we are done with the appointments. My mother didn't ask for me to take anything she just contacted a driver to come and pick us up, we said goodbye to everyone in the house and she held my hand and we went into the taxi and drove away. I sat in the car and lay my head on my mother's chest, she started crying bitterly, I know that she was feeling guilty because she then picked up the phone and called Rakie and explained the state that she found me in and how much she regrets trusting these people.

We arrived at the Senegambia Hotel which was located at the more tourist led side of Gambia. The place was so beautiful it was like paradise, high ceilings with planted palm trees with waiters and waitresses passing by in their crisp white shirts. We got to our hotel room and my mother prepared a hot bubble bath and poured some dettol in there, she put me in and scrubbed my body clean. After my bath my mother took out some new princess pajamas that she brought for me for wear and ordered some dinner for us from room service. When my burger and chips came I ate like I had never been fed before and my mother sat and watched me and cried. We spent the evening with me filling in her with everything that had happened and my mother spent the rest of the night on the phone to family and friends in Manchester crying and narrating what had happened, I was so tired so that I dosed off. I opened my eyes and it was morning, the sun was shining so bright and the palm trees stood tall outside our hotel room. My mother was sat down on a chair opposite the bed smiling and told me good morning; she told me that she could tell that I was tired that's why she left me to sleep. She bathed me again and put some clothes on me, it felt good to wear new underwear again and shoes that didn't hurt when I walked. She brushed out my hair and we left to go and have breakfast. Senegambia's breakfasts is one of the best, I was spoilt for choice so I took everything, fruit, cereal, toast and ham, I had it all because I deserved it after the two years of suffering I had gone through.

I later found out that our appointment at the British embassy wasn't the next day but the day after, my mother just wanted to take me away with her instantly. We went for our appointment and straight away I was given my visa to travel, my mother immediately made arrangements for my ticket to be purchased and we would leave Gambia the following week. We went back to see Aunty A and her family and off course they were all covered with shame. When they saw how good I looked with my fresh clothes and braided hair, they even told me that I was a beautiful girl as if I

wasn't beautiful before or was it my beauty
that scared them to make them want to
degrade me. I introduced my mum to Hajah's
family and she showed them her gratitude with
some money and gave some of my clothes to
Hajah. Hajah told me not to forget her and we
promised to be friends forever no matter the
distance. We went to go and see Adama and
her family but it was the summer holidays and
the whole family had travelled to the USA
which saddened me because I really wanted to
say goodbye. I was going to miss Adama and
Hajah just like I missed Jeneba and they would
all hold a special place in my heart. We spent
our last week enjoying Gambia, visiting my
mother's friends and dining and exploring
Banjul. A week later there I was at Banjul
international airport with my mother beside me
as we prepared to board a plane to
Manchester, I looked back at the airport and
apart me felt sad; I was happy but I was sad
because I wondered how Jeneba was doing, if
she had started school and If she still cried
during shower time. I thought about Hajah and
if they would ever have enough money for her
to go to school. Each step that I took towards
that plane was a step away from the bitterness
I tasted in Gambia, I started remembering all

the days that I prayed to God to rescue me from what felt like hell to me and finally he answered and I was on my way home. As beautiful as a country like Gambia is, I tasted the worst of it; a taste that stayed in my mouth for years but never did it strive me from remembering and loving the people that brought sunshine to my rainy days on the shores of Gambia.

5 HOME SWEET HOME

Returning back home to Manchester was the
most amazing feeling in the world, all my
family came to welcome me back, cousins and
aunts and uncles that I did not recognise at all.
The first few days felt so unreal, as I walked
around my area friends from my childhood
screamed with joy when they saw me; the
worst feeling was having to pretend I
remembered people that I didn't remember. I
started to adjust to life back in the UK, my
mother was so surprised at how trained I was
with domestic work but then again when you
spend a few years in the role of the help all the
tasks become natural to you. At this point in
time I was 11 years old, I had celebrated my
birthday in Gambia a few days before we
travelled so on my return to Manchester it was
time to get me ready for high school in
September. I spent the summer working with
my mother and some days I was either with my
cousins or at home with my sister Rakie who
was living away from home at the time. As
summer came to an end my mother and sister
started prepping me for high school, rules and

regulations about academics were put into place and my mother made it very clear that I was to stay away from boys at all cost, the fact that she enrolled me in an all girls school speaks volumes. September came by so quickly and it was time for me to start school, I was so nervous, school was something that I had wanted for so long so I was looking forward to starting without any interruptions.

My first day of school was scary, I was all dressed in my black skirt with black tights, white shirt, purple tie and black blazer, my mother took so many pictures and my sister took me to school for my first day and told me she would pick me up after school. We walked to school because it was only a 10 minute drive from where we lived so walking wasn't really a far distance. I got to the school gates and my sister wished me luck and waved goodbye and there I was finally facing the future I deserved. I met my first set of friends that day, they were two Muslim girls from Sudan called Jamila and Khadijah, and they both wore hijabs and were very much committed to their faith and culture even at that tender age of just being 11 years old. I met other friends but I bonded more with Jamila and Khadijah and they became my best friends in school for the next three years.

The hardest part of adjusting back into my life in the UK was high school, as much as I had loved coming back home and reconnecting with my family and friends the transition wasn't as easy as I thought it would be because I didn't realise that I returned home with emotional baggage. The first year was okay, I spent most of my time with my family while I adjusted into the new relationships I was building in school and reconnecting with my old primary school friends. I came to realise that there was this big divide when it came to culture, coming from an African background and being raised in an English culture was very confusing and distressing at times. I went to an all girl's school which was rated as one of the best public schools in Manchester at the time; we had a mixture of a lot of cultures and religions but no matter how great a school is nothing can prevent the chronicles of peer pressure. The second year of high came by quickly and suddenly I started to show signs of the pressure I was feeling, as bold as I was as a child I became so withdrawn; I don't know where my voice went but I came to realise that

some of the traumatic events that had
happened to be a few years back affected me
in ways that I couldn't put into words. At home
I was Fatmata, I could smile freely and dance
around the house and speak loudly without
wondering what everyone else thought, but
once I got to those school gates something
would change and I would just shut down. I
think it started when sex education classes
started at school, that's the only time I
remember that something inside of me started
to change and I became withdrawn. I didn't
realise the impact of what had happened to me,
it was as if a part of me thought that being
abused was all a part of the process of growing
up. Every time they would start talking about
sex in the class room I would start having flash
backs, my body would start getting hot and I
would put my head down into my desk as I try
to catch my breath. Some days I wouldn't be
able to sit through the conversation, I would
peacefully walk out of the class room and find
a corner to cry and in those moments I started
to realise just how much I was violated. I had
two views about what I thought sex was, the
first view was that sex was this beautiful and
sexy thing that should be shared between two
people who loved each other, two people who

were off age and both consulting the sex. The second view I had was that it was a horrific disgusting act, it was dark and bitter and there was nothing special or bonding about it, it was the act that darkened your soul and left you with emotional wounds.

I did my best to blank out the memories and try and live a normal teenage life, I had a mother that though she loved me very much she was wrapped up in her role of being the only bread winner for our family. My siblings were all grown and living their lives, Lamin was in the Army but was still living at home and Rashida was a Air Hostess with virgin Atlantic but she lived with us as and when but most times she had her own place. Rakie was studying at Bolton University and Abdul lived on the other side of Manchester and was in the process of opening his food business. The family wasn't perfect but we were okay at this time, we spent Christmas holidays together and celebrated birthdays; we did the things that normal families did especially the sibling fights and rivalry, that was an everyday episode in our household. At this time I was fourteen years old and everything was changing, my body was developing and it was developing very quickly, my hips spread and my breast started to form something that I was never comfortable with. My mother had the talk with me, you know the talk about the birds and the bees but she gave me the African parent threat version where she told me that no boy should ever touch my breast or my private part; she even went a step further by putting African waist beads on me and told me that those beads were magical and if a boy ever touched me she would know. During that conversation I felt sick to the pit of my stomach, I felt disgusting and unclean because more and more as the years passed by I was reminded just how much of a big deal sex was and there I was sitting in front of my mother who was trying to find ways of preventing me from giving away my virginity not knowing that it had already been taken away long before she could even comprehend.

My mother was still working as a market trader so on weekends I would have to work with her; I absolutely hated doing it especially during the winter. I did always admire her strength though, no matter how late she went to bed or how late she returned from going out somewhere my mother made sure she was always ready by 5am to leave the house for work. Most market traders depending on the markets they sell at would have to be set up and ready by 7am. It wasn't all bad because with my mother's job came the privileges of always having lots of shoes and clothes and most of the latest fashion must haves but back then I don't think I appreciated it as much. I was fortunate because my mother taught me from a very young age to be independent and to be able to work for whatever I wanted or needed. Because my mother knew how much I hated spending my weekends working with her she started teaching me independence and started paying me for my work because at this time I was a teenager and I was missing out on time to socialise with my friends while I was working with her. My mother started paying me £20 a day, back then for an almost fourteen year old that was a lot of money. Because all of my needs were met by my mother I saved the money that my mother paid me to buy the extra things that my mother refused to buy for me. At this time there were also privileges that came with Rashida's job, she was now working for Air Atlantic and their route was Manchester to Florida and family members and friends got one free ticket and got to travel with them to

Florida for a week and off course I was the first to benefit. The day my mother told me I was going I was so excited I wanted to jump into the sky and that was the first of many trips that I would take to the USA.

Going to an all girls school was not as great as some parents think it will be, they say it is less of a distraction with boys around but the reality was that we were so hormonal and boy hungry that a high percentage of the girls in our school had been pregnant and had several abortions before they turned sixteen. We knew the ones that were sexually active because during our sex education classes some of our friends became our teachers. I was lucky to have a diverse group of friends; I was friends with the black girls, the Asian girls, the white girls and the biracial girls that had a squad of their own at times. I just loved people and whoever made me laugh I loved to be around so I was the easy going person in every group. At the age of fourteen things became really intense for me in school because of a group of black girls who were horrible to me. Their names were Chantelle and Sharene, they made the next year of my life in high school so unbearable. It started with me walking past them and they would giggle and for the longest time I ignored and told myself that it was their private joke and most times I would take the longer routes around the school just to avoid them and no matter how hard I tried by the end of the school day I would still encounter them and that became the worst feeling for me.

For the longest time I didn't speak up about what was going on because I didn't want to come across like a cry baby and I truly believed that it was phase that they were going through and soon enough they would find a new target to bully. During this time destiny's child was the girl group that every young black teenager around the world looked up too, they represented the minorities and they stood for everything that they said a black woman couldn't be. I loved beyonce, she inspired me so much and at that point I wanted to wear everything I saw her wearing on a limited teenage girl budget. There was this big bouncy curly hair style that beyonce did in the bootilicious music video that I feel in love with and begged my mother to pay for me to have it done and off course she agreed. I went into school with my head held high with my new hairstyle; to be fair I looked more like a poodle

than I did beyonce because I could only afford
synthetic hair at that time so you can only
imagine the difference in mine and beyonce's
hair. I spent the day with all my friends telling
me how good my hair looked and whether they
lied or not I didn't care I was just happy to
have that hair style and off course wherever
there is light darkness will try to enter. I was
walking down a hallway in school during lunch
time and there they were walking towards me,
Sharene and Chantelle, my heart was beating
really fast and I prayed in my heart that they
wouldn't say anything to me. I walked bravely
and engaged in conversation with my two
friends and as they noticed me they whispered
to each other for a few seconds and as they
got nearer they burst into laughter and started
pointing at me saying "Omgosh she looks more
like Christina Aguilera than beyonce ", I was so
embarrassed and my heart fell as I continued
to walk with my friends who advised me to just
ignore them. I went home that day with a
bruised ego and spent the next few weeks
being named and shamed by these girls and
every day I would ask myself what I did wrong,
I started hating school and every morning when
I woke up and thought about what I had to face
my heart would start feeling heavy straight

away. Some days I would spend my time in the bathroom crying before I had my bath because I couldn't cry while I was at school or cry at home around my family because they would notice that something was wrong. My friends in school told me to speak up and say something to the teachers but I didn't want to come across as weak and attract more people that would want to start bullying me. I was really going through it; this was a stage in my life where I was trying to figure out who I was and how I felt about myself. The boys in my area also started making fun of how I looked, they teased me because of my lips which they called " rubber lips ", my body developed quicker and my shape blossomed as my hips spread; I hated every part of myself because they told me that I wasn't pretty. My lips were much fuller than my white friends, I could never find jeans that fit my structure so I wore a lot of tights which revealed my shape even more and that made me feel more insecure. Apart from my mother and other families members I didn't see people that represented me in the world around me so I started to believe everything that they told me, I started wishing that I looked like the biracial girls and Caucasians girls who had the beautiful hair and slim figures.

As I became a teenager it became harder for me to talk to my mother, she was different with how she reasoned and to be honest she was always busy fending for the family so there was hardly much time for structured parenting as far as I was concerned. My sister Rakie did all the mothering when it came to me because most times my mother was either out of the country or working on her businesses. My sister was everything rolled into one for me, Rakie was my cook, my doctor, my comedian and ultimately she was my mother. I was always so happy when she would come home for weekends and I especially loved the time we would spend together when our mother travelled. Rakie taught me how to make club sandwiches and shop on a budget, something that really helped me later on in life. Speaking to my sister about what was going on at school was hard because I didn't even want to accept that what was happening was real, it felt like Gambia all over again but this time I had my family to lean on but I chose not to.

I found it easier to speak to my Aunty Fatu; she has a calmness about her that just made me feel secure and safe to share what I was feeling. I went to visit her one day and as we spoke about school and everything else I opened up and cried and told her everything that was going on and she asked me why I didn't tell my mother and to that question I didn't really have an answer but the reality was that my mother would have solved the issue but I didn't want her to do it in a way that would make things more difficult for me at school. Aunty Fatu called my mother and told her everything and my mother shared that information with Rakie and they both sat me down when I returned home and asked me what was going on and I broke down and cried bitterly about what had been going on in school and how the boys around our area were also teasing me about how I looked. My mother had this deep look of sorrow in her eyes as I cried, almost like she wanted to cry but held it in. My mother held my hand and said to me "Look at me Fatmata ", I wiped my tears and looked up at her and with so much strength in her voice she said "Fatmata you are more beautiful than you know, everything about you is unique and beautiful; the things that they are laughing at you now for will be what the world will later praise you for ". I didn't understand and couldn't accept what she was saying because how could the world ever love me when I looked how I looked, I wasn't beautiful, my lips were so big and my hips spread and my bum was just uncontrollable that I hated the idea of who I was. My mother told me that I cannot allow anyone to tell me what I should love and hate about myself because I was beautiful regardless. she told me that I may not see it now but one day I would realise that it is actually my beauty that scares them and that's why they tease me and laugh at me because they want to break my confidence. At that point I was so unhappy that I told my mother that I wanted to move to another school because I refused to return to school if I had to keep dealing with Chantelle and Sharene. My mother immediately made an appointment with my school's head teacher and went and addressed the issue with them and she did not take it very lightly. My mother told them that Chantelle and Sharene should be dealt with immediately otherwise she would take matters into her own hands and it would not be a beautiful picture for them. My mother became the parent that they knew that did not accept foolish behavior; she was straight to the point and always wanted to break the school protocols if something didn't favour her. I remember a time when I had been placed on a negative report system for bad behavior which meant I spent my lunch times and after schools in detention. I served my 2 week sentence and then I got into trouble at school again and I was placed back onto the lunch time and after school detention.

My mother was very angry and frustrated because normally after school is when I do some of my daily tasks at home and run errands for her in our local area. I was sitting in after school detention on the fourth day and the phone rang, the entire room was silent and the teacher that was there picked up the phone and whether it was the fact that my mother was loud of that the volume on the phone was high but we heard was a high pitched voice shouting on the other side of the phone and the teacher saying " No Mrs Bockari we can't do that, if you just calm down I can maybe explain " we heard muffles for the next few minutes while the teacher's temperature seemed to be rising and then all we heard was " okay Mrs Bockari we will send her home ". The teacher called my name and told me to go home that my mother needed me to do something, the entire classroom erupted into laughter; that was who my mother was, she held no prisoners and was never afraid to command what she wanted and that particular situation made her the topic of my school for that week, people would walk over to me and say " Yo your mum is a G ", and on parents evening they were all so excited to meet her.

The issue with Chantelle and Sharene was addressed by my school and they were warned but off course they didn't listen to what was said so they confronted me screaming and shouting until some of the other students and teacher had to separate the incident and from that moment they had to stop because then they were in trouble and a second warning and a call home to parents tends to keep people in check. They would see me at school and not say a word to me but if eyes could kill that would have been a different story. I did my best to move past that stage and tried to make new friends in school, I became very involved in sports so I spent a lot of time training with my PE teachers; I joined some after school sport clubs such as the rugby and athletics club and met a lot of new friends through that which kept me occupied. I had finally found something that I loved, If I wasn't doing sports I was busy

writing in my books, building my characters
and making up stories. I loved being in that
world of fantasy where I could just disappear
and get wrapped up in a world that I created
with my words. I started reading and I enjoyed
it just as much as I did as doing sports and
writing stories. I was fifteen years old now and
I was doing well in school socially but
struggling a little academically, as the years
passed it seemed like more of traumatic
experiences kept coming back to remind me of
my pain and I didn't deal with that very well. I
started getting into fights at school, I wasn't
the one starting them but definitely I was
defending myself. I became so fearless driven
by anger and pain but I made them all believe
that it was strength. Things turned upside
down for me when a friend of mine was
brutally raped by two boys she considered to
be her friends. It hit me hard and I guess I just
lost it, I became enraged and I wanted justice
for her and for myself and I just didn't know
what I could do. My behavior became so bad
that I was taken out of class every single day
and I didn't care that it was happening, I didn't
care that my mother was upset about it, all I
cared about was the fact that for that particular
moment I could cause distress to someone else

and they would have to carry what I had been carrying for so long but I had nowhere to offload. I started hanging around with the bad kids in my area and that did not go down well with my mother and I didn't care at all. I started smoking with them and drinking with them and it felt so good to feel like I was in control and it was a better feeling than the rottenness and the dirty feeling I had every time I would have flashbacks about what my Uncle did to me. I was called at school to have a private meeting with one of the heads of the schools that I had a very close bond with, her name was Ms McClean, she was one of my favorite teachers, and she really understood me and how to deal with me. Ms McClean called me to her office for a one to one conversation and told me that she didn't like the version of me that she was witnessing and asked me what was going on with me. I told her that I was okay and that there was nothing wrong and she told me that people normally act out when they are trying to cover something up that they don't want to deal with and she told me that she could only help me if I shared whatever it was that was bothering me. For the first time in a long I felt as though somebody heard my cry and noticed that my behavior was actually a cry for help. I opened up and told her what had happened to me back in Sierra Leone and how I was trying to forget about it but I just couldn't. Ms McClean held my hand and told me that I wasn't just suppose to forget about it because I was violated, she told me that I was very strong to have kept that to myself for so long and promised me that she would do whatever it took to make sure I got all the support I needed. Ms McClean also told me that because I had made that disclosure at school she needed to inform the school about what I had said and also inform my mother and straight away and I started crying. I begged her not to tell my mother because it would cause too many issues in my family especially if my father was told I didn't want to be the one that broke the family bond. Ms McClean reassured me that there was nothing for me to be afraid off and the only way I would ever be free for it was to speak about it and address the issue and not keep those feelings wrapped up.

My mother was called to the school by Ms McClean to have the discussion about what I had disclosed. I approached Ms McClean before they arrived and told her that I didn't want to tell my mother anymore, she told me

that I was just afraid and needed to go ahead
and tell her. A few days before my mother had
caught me smoking and beat me silly, her and
Rakie were so disappointed and I didn't want to
tell them because they would have thought that
I only spoke up about my abuse because I was
already in trouble for smoking and that wasn't
the case but they believed that anyway. Ms
McClean shared the news with my mother and
sister, she spoke slowly and she kept her eyes
on me as she spoke, my eyes were down to the
floor because I was too ashamed and afraid to
look at my mother or my sister. When Ms
McClean finally told them all I heard was sobs
and then crying from both my mother and
sister and then my mother asked me "Fatmata
is this true ", I looked up and shook my head
and instantly my mother opened her arms to
hug me as she cried, I started crying because I
hated it when my mother cried. Rakie was
distraught, I could see the pain in her eyes, and
Ms McClean gave us some privacy while my
mother and Rakie asked me why I didn't tell
them and started asking me questions that I
wasn't ready to answer. The meeting ended
and Ms McClean advised that I be put forward
for school counselling and also extra tutor
support during the sex education classes which

seemed to me a trigger for me and also
suggested that I be removed from those
classes until I was ready to return. Ms McClean
was a saint in my eyes; she was my savor who
helped me to cross a bridge that I was so
afraid to walk across. I went home after school
and met my mother and sister waiting for me in
the kitchen, the kitchen is where we spent
most of our time. We had a big long kitchen
with a great dining space, I went in and sat by
my sister and put my school bag on the floor.
My mother and sister started shooting
questions at me one after the other and as I
answered the more my mother would cry. My
mother apologised to me for leaving me in
Sierra Leone for so long and said that if she
knew that anything like this was happening she
would have brought me back sooner. We
spoke for a while after that and for the next
few days things were a little awkward in the
house, maybe not to them but it was for me. I
felt as though I was walking with a sign on my
head with my deepest secretes being spilled to
the entire world. I pushed myself through those
counselling sessions; I did a lot of crying and
made sense of how I felt about the abuse. I
realised that my anger was the reaction to my
abuse, I was angry at him, at my mother and at

my father because I didn't feel like they did enough to protect me but I didn't want to hurt them by being vocal about that because I already knew that my mother felt guilt. She begged me not to ever speak of it to my father because it would break his heart and by this time my father was dealing with the destruction of the Bockari dynasty and that within itself were coals of fire underneath our feet. .

6 KNOCKING ON HEAVEN'S DOOR

My life was settled and I was living like most teenage girls my age, my mother was still travelling and doing her business and Rakie was back at home caring for me when my mother was away. I was fully focused on my sports and my writing, it became my life; I spent my pocket money and money I got from working with my mother buying empty A4 books and in every book I created my stories and my characters. I wrote so much that it almost felt like I was living in another world, I created the characters that I wanted to be and the worlds I imagine that I could escape too. I had received news that my father had a political case, accusations were made against him and through this he lost him position and was sent to jail. People expected that I would defend my father because he was my father but the reality was that I defended him because the truth was the truth and the truth was that he did not do what he was accused off but when you trust a dozen snakes how can you expect not to be bitten. My father was sentenced and when my mother informed me I remember crying so much because I couldn't make sense of it, how could a man that was so great be driven down to such destruction. My father was a victim of his own faults, he was too kind and too trusting and those that wanted to bring him down knew that so they did what they did and he fell. People said so much horrible things about our family; they called us all thieves and mocked the younger children when they would go to school or college. I made sure that I said prayers for him and I pray that God would fight for him and get him justice.

I had inherited the gift of running from my father, all the Bockari children were known to be good at sports, and I remember my father winning all the parent races when I was in primary school. So as a teenager I embraced that talent, nothing gave me more joy than when I was running, I don't know if it was the breeze or the feeling that running gave me; it made me feel like I was so fearless. My PE teachers took special interest in me when I had broken records at my school, I beat the running time of all my sport teachers and they told me that I was so good that I could make it to the Olympics. I trained every day after school whether the teachers were there or not I still trained, I would get one of my friends to time me and I would send my timings to my sport teachers. I joined the tag rugby team and did so well because of how fast I was, I represented my school and competed in local tournaments. Every year I would beg my mother to come and watch me run but she never did because she was always busy travelling or working but she always saw all the medals and certificates I brought home after my competitions. I took my sports so seriously that I stopped socialising with friends on weekends so I could attend extra training sessions, it became so serious for me because I really wanted to do something that would make my father proud because once I told him that I was doing sports and training he was so happy and proud. I wanted to go to the Olympics and win a medal for England and take that medal to Sierra Leone to lay it in my father's palms just to remind him that he was still great because I would always do whatever it took to make him proud. My sport teachers arranged a meeting with my mother to discuss taking my athletics to the next level, I was so happy because an Olympic trainer had seen me run and wanted to train me to compete nationally. My teachers told my mother that all she needed to do was consent for me to start the training camp and the rest would be done through sponsorship. My mother refused, she told them that I was the daughter and niece of political minister, I come from a family of politicians and graduates so her plan for me was to finish school, go to college and then university and if I were to start training and make it professionally as an athlete I would abandon my studies. My sport teachers pleaded with my mother but she refused and she was adamant that I would not train professionally and needed to focus on my studies. I was heartbroken, for weeks I walked around with a heavy heart and even bought a special book for my mother and every day I would write about how much I hated her for what she did to me and this was the beginning of what were the challenging years of my teenage life.

I continued to train at school, although I couldn't take it any further I still took joy in the countless awards I won for my athletic achievements and finally I got the chance to meet my sports hero Dennis Lewis at a sporting event and I told her how much I admired her and wanted to run like her in the Olympics one day. She gave me some good pointers and told me that if I trained hard enough and wanted it enough I would make it as long as I never lost hope. That advice meant everything to me but it fell on empty ground because my mother had already made a decision for me and I had no choice but to swallow that bullet and find a career that pleased her. The year before I left school was so intense; I had gone from being this timid quite girl to being troublesome. I was getting in trouble every month and coming home with bad reports, my mother would scream and shout and threaten to send me back to Sierra Leone to live with my father but I didn't really care because as far as I was concerned what else could happen to me that hadn't already happened. My innocence was already taken, I had been beaten and abused in every way possible, I had been told that I was ugly and unloved so there was nothing left for the world to do to me that had not been already done so her threats were empty. My pre-calculated grades for my GCSE's were bad and my mother was surprised and disappointed, I was happy because that was a part of my life that I could control, I wanted to be an athlete, and I wanted to write and it seemed as though no one could hear me so I decided that I was going to close my mind to everything else and that reflected in my school grades. I had taken business as a major that was an additional level 3 qualification and that was my strong point and I was predicted a distinction grade which meant even if I didn't get enough GSCE's my business qualification would still push me forward to college and that was my mother's saving grace.

School became my safe haven, my friends became my family; at school I got to deal with my issues whether it was through sports or through the daily laughter I would share with my friends but I got to just forget about everything that was weighing on my mind and just be a teenager. I remember coming home from school one day and seeing my mother sitting down on the chair in the living room with a letter in her hand and asked me to come and sit next to her, I asked her what was wrong and the exhaled as she held my hand and told me that she received news from Sierra Leone that my grandmother mama Hawa had passed away. Immediately broke down and started crying as my mother embraced me and told me that it was going to be okay, I cried and cried as I imagined her small frail lifeless body and how much I wanted to be in her arms again. Earlier that day when I was having my bath to get ready for school I actually saw my grandmother walk past and I screamed and told my mother what I saw but she just assumed that I was imagining things so as she held me crying I knew that she had come to say goodbye to me. Just like many of the other things weighing heavy on my heart the news of my grandmother's death almost pushed me over the edge. I was dealing with my identity, my insecurities, making sense of the abuse I had been through and still trying to understand what it meant to be a young woman growing up as my body was developing; I was growing hips, thighs and breast and I didn't look like most of my friends. I started making myself vomit every time I had food to eat I would find the toilet at school and put my fingers down my throat and vomit out everything that I had eaten. I had read that this was something that a lot of young girls did to lose weight and it worked for them and I was over weight for my age and I wanted to fit into size six or eight trousers and not have to wear a size ten. I did this for about a month and I started to see the results and I was happy because nobody had noticed. One day I was in class and I asked the teacher if I could go to the toilet, she allowed me and I went and made myself vomit and came back into class. My friend Sharrelle who was sitting two chairs down from me passed me a note which said "did you go to the toilet to make yourself sick ", I was so shocked because I didn't know how she found out; so I wrote a note back to her and asked her how she knew and she told me that she had been watching for the past few days and noticed what was going on. Sharrelle wrote me a long note telling me how dangerous what I was doing was and told me that I was fine just the way I was and I didn't need to look like anyone else. Her exact words were "You don't need to look like no bumerclart white gyal yeah ". Sharrelle was the comedian of our group, so getting such seriousness from her showed me just how much she cared and being that she was the only one to notice spoke volumes.

For the next week days sharrelle watched and followed me closely during lunch time to make sure I wouldn't go and make myself sick and I didn't do it at school anymore but I continued at home for about another month until I finally stopped because I didn't have to make myself vomit anymore it started happening automatically whenever I ate and my mother thought that I was pregnant. She took me to the doctor to have a pregnancy test done because she didn't believe me when I told her that I wasn't pregnant. When the test returned negative the doctor asked my mother leave the room and spoke to me about Bulimia which he said was a mental health eating disorder and told me about the risks and the long term consequences. The doctor didn't share this information with my mother but I was informed me that my school would be informed as I had told my doctor that I was already in counselling and telling my mother would only add more stress to my life, instead I promised to speak to my counsellor about it and ask for additional support.

My school days were over and I had successfully started college, I was 16 years old and at this point it seemed as though everything was settled. My mother was still travelling and our relationship had become more strained. I had left home a few times because we struggled to see eye to eye and my mother didn't really understand me. I had a closer relationship with my sister Rakie who was my mother figure most of the time, Lamin was still in the army, Rashida was still working with airlines and Abdul was working and pursuing his music. We weren't the best and most united family but we co-existed when we needed too which were birthdays, holidays and special family occasions that we all needed to attend. My mother started getting unwell, she travelled so much that we just assumed that it was her body giving her a sign that she needed to slow down. She had asthma and at one point she had been diagnosed with an enlarged heart. She returned home and told us the news and she cried for so long. Me and Rakie didn't fully understand why she was crying because we believed that it wasn't the end of her life and advised her to take the doctor's advice and slow down with the work and travelling. She seemed to listen and totally did a 360, she was different; she was more attentive and supportive and started telling me how proud she was of me and how much she loved me. My mother was telling me that I needed to work hard to make sure I made my father proud and told me to never forget him no matter what happened, I told her to stop speaking as if she was about to die and reminded her that she was totally fine. On another day she sat me and Rakie down in the kitchen and told us that she wanted us to have a heart to heart about something; my mother apologised for not being the best version of herself and told us that she did the best that she could according to what she was taught about being mother. She told us that when she was a teenager she was raped, she spoke without any emotion as if she felt nothing, she spoke about being raised by her grandmother and not her mother and how that affected her emotionally. She disclosed many things that caused me and my Rakie to hug her and cry because she couldn't cry for herself, she was so built on being this iron lady that she always thought that she had flesh that could easily be torn and in that moment for the first time we realised that her life was also a consequence of trauma. She apologised to me for not protecting me from being abused and said that her worst nightmare had come to light because she had prayed that none of her children would have to go through what she did. I thought about the amount of aunties that maybe have had this same experience and never spoke out about it because they believed their voice was never loud enough to be heard and this was something I wanted to change in the African culture.

It was now July 2006, I was about to turn

seventeen and my mother had promised that I could have a party to celebrate because I had wanted one for so long. I started planning and my mother even gave me the deposit for the venue. I told all my friends in college and me, my cousins and friends couldn't wait for the day to finally arrive because this was one of the first teenage occasions of my life that my mother was in full support off. Abdul had gotten married and had a son with his wife who was living in Gambia at the time, He had made arrangements for his wife and my nephew Jamal to come and join him in the UK. Rakie supported Abdul and went with him to London Heathrow to pick up his wife and son; I was at home with my mother who at the time was having constant asthma attacks. One night it was around eleven thirty at night and I was asleep when my mother banged my door open and I scared awake and saw her standing by my door breathless. I quickly ran and took her back into her room and found her inhalers while I tried to stabilise her but this time it didn't work and it seemed as though it was getting worse and her breathing was getting out of control. I called 999 and asked for an ambulance and within ten minutes they came to the house and hooked my mother on an oxygen

machine. We were taken to Manchester Royal
infirmary hospital and they asked me to stay in
the waiting room as they took her into the
emergency room. I sat there with my mother's
bag in my arms and I called Rakie and Abdul
and told them what was happening, they were
in London and told me to keep them updated as
they would be driving back to Manchester as
soon as possible. I sat in that waiting room for
other four hours until the waiting room was
empty and then around 3.30am two doctors
came and called me and took me into a private
room and sat me down. First they asked me
how old I was and I told them that I was 16 but
would be 17 in two weeks. They asked me if I
had any other family that could come to the
hospital and I told them that my elder siblings
are in London and would be coming back in the
morning. One of the doctors bend down on one
knee and looked directly in my eyes and
started explaining to me things and words that
I didn't understand, I blanked out and just
focused on his eyes and his eyes told me that
everything wasn't okay. He spoke slowly and
my heart was beating really fast, I only heard
him say was that my mother had been
stabilised and that they had placed her on a
ventilator that would assist her with her

breathing. They said that she had been taken to one of the wards and asked me If I wanted to see her and I said yes. As I walked and followed one of the doctors all types of thoughts were going through my mind and the worst was the one that I refused to believe because, I told myself that my mother was going to be fine and she would beat this and make it home again.

We reached the entrance of the ward, there it was the sign that read "Intensive care", at that moment I still didn't gasp what was happening, so I cleaned my hands with the sanitizer and followed the doctor. We walked in and I saw so many machines so many lifeless bodies on bed, I was in total shock and my heart was beating really fast. We walked to the end of the room and at the last bed on the left I saw my mother, I took one look at her and burst into tears; she was lifeless with a machine breathing for her and there was this long pipe that went through her throat that was connected to the ventilator. The doctor came nearer and comforted me and gave me some tissue to wipe my tears, he told me that I could stay with her for a little while but I would need to leave and come back in the morning during visiting hours. I sat beside her and held her hand and cried, I told her that what I was seeing didn't look good and I begged her to fight it and come back to me; I started apologising to her for all my bad behavior and I promised that if she got better I would do whatever she asked without complaining. I cried so much that I dozed off holding her hand to my cheek as I leaned on her bed. A nurse came and woke me up and told me that I should go home and come back in a few hours so I got up and looked her and felt so guilty because I didn't want to leave her there alone, I wanted to sleep by her side but I had no choice so I had to leave. I called Rakie and Abdul and told them what had happened and they were on their way back to Manchester, I walked out of hospital and got a night bus home and it felt like the longest and loneliest journeys ever.

The next day we all gathered by her bed side, Rakie and Abdul had spoken to the doctors and they informed us that at this point it was a 50/50 chance, either she would pull through or she wouldn't and we were not prepared for the second option. Our family members were contacted and slowly they started to arrive to support us, we took it in turns to be by our mother's bed side, it was mostly between me and Rakie for the first week. We prayed over her and read the psalms of David, pastors came and family members came and well prayed, she was alert and she could hear everything we were saying she just couldn't communicate is what we were told. The day of my birthday came, Rakie gave me some money and my friends took me out for dinner to lift up my spirit, It was a lovely and kind gesture but at the back of my mind I kept thinking about my mother and how we had planned my 17th birthday celebration and there I was sitting down surrounded by friends who loved me but all I wanted was my mother. The day after my birthday I went to the hospital to see my mother, I stood over her and watched as the machine calculated every type of circulation in her body, I started talking to her, I told her that I was now seventeen and that I went out with my friends for my birthday but I missed spending my birthdays with her and in that moment tears started to roll down my mother's lifeless face and I knew that she could hear me; it gave me hope and I thought that she would pull through so I continued to talk to her and told her that life wouldn't make sense without her because the two week had been the worst week of our lives. We continued to pray and took it in turns to sit by her bed side, Lamin had returned from the army but Rashida was in America but was sent back as soon as we contacted her airline to tell them what had happened. She returned but didn't come to the hospital straight away and that angered me because I couldn't make sense of it, there is nothing more important than the life of our mother but I guess buying her first car was her priority. The doctors started to reduce the percentage of likeliness that our mother would recover fully but we remained faithful and continued to believe that God would heal her.

It was Saturday July 25th 2006 and it was the day off the Manchester carnival, I will never forget that day because as much as the sun was shining it was also raining. My friends came to my house and told me that we should go to the carnival and I told them that I couldn't because I wanted to go to the hospital, they encouraged to go with them to get my mind off everything and with everything that was going on I think I needed to just take my mind off reading psalms and talking to doctors and crying at hospital bed sides, I just needed to be in a space of joy and not sorrow. I made sure that my phone was charged and had told my friends that I would go to the hospital straight after since the park wasn't far away. I got to the carnival and it wasn't fun, I smiled and I laughed but my heart was heavy, I kept my phone in my bag and something told me to check it, so I opened my bag and took my phone out and there I saw twenty five missed calls from Lamin and from my cousin little John. My heart started beating really fast and in that moment I got another call from my cousin John and I answered and asked what was wrong and he told me that I needed to come to the hospital and asked where I was, I froze and ended the call and my friends asked me what was wrong and I told them that I needed to go home something was wrong and straight away I started running and as I was running I was crying; I got on the bus and received another call from Lamin and he asked where I was and I told him that I was on my way home and he told me he was coming to get me.

I rushed home and changed my clothes and kept wondering what would have happened but I told myself that It wasn't what I was thinking because I knew it hadn't come to that yet. I sat at the edge of the stairs at home as I waited for Lamina to come and pick me up and in that short moment I started imagining the worst and started telling myself to stop thinking negatively maybe the doctors needed to give us an update and things couldn't have gotten that bad in the past few hours. Lamin came with one of his friends and picked me up, there was small talk in the car but one thing was very clear and that was the tension, we got to the hospital and me and Lamin walked to the intensive care unit and as we walked Lamin put his arm around me and said "Don't worry Fatmata I promise that were going to look after you ", I ignored his statement because I refused to accept the reality of what seemed to be happening. We walked into the ward and I started seeing family members gathered outside the waiting room, I saw Uncle Akie who was my siblings dad and he gave me a hug, some cousins and aunties were there, I greeted them and walked past everyone to go into the family room and as I walked in I saw Rashida sitting in front of me with a room full of people and as she saw me she burst into tears and I also started crying, everyone in the room started crying once they saw us cry and in that moment I finally had to accept it. I cried for a while as I was comforted by my family and we were told that our mother would not be able to breathe without the ventilator supporting her and that there was nothing more they could do and asked us as a family to make a decision on whether or not we wanted to turn the ventilator off. The decision was left to my step father Uncle Akie since he stepped in as her husband it was decided that the machine would be turned off.

We gathered at her bed side around 8.30pm on July 25th and prayers were said, speeches were made and my heart ached. I kept looking at the machine that showed her heart rate and kept praying that God would intervene. I stood by her side and cried and whispered as I begged and begged and pleaded with her not to leave, I was ready to give up everything and in that moment I started regretting every argument we had ever had and every time I thought I hated her; all I wanted was for her to wake up and tell me that everything was going to be okay. They turned the ventilator off and we all and watched as her heart rate dropped and we all cried but there was nothing more painful than the sound of that last beep which was the sound of her heart failing, I fell to the ground crying in agony, for the first I understood what they mean when they say the heartaches, my heart ached so badly and I became breathless. Rashida picked me up from the floor and hugged me so tight but the pain didn't go away, my whole body was numb, we sat in the family room as arrangements were made for my mother's body and my friends came, they all embraced me and we all cried; I cried like a baby because my world had fallen apart and in those moments I questioned the world and wondered if I was dreaming because none of this felt real. The drive home was painful, my cousin Hadiza was driving my mother's Audi, and she was so proud of that car when she bought it and to imagine that now she wasn't even around to drive it anymore. We got to the house and the door was opened, the house was as cold as ice, I felt this breeze of sorrow and loneliness; I walked up the stairs and went straight to my mother's room and stood and gazed at her empty bed and I lost it again and broke down into tears. "Mummy why would you do this to me, why would you leave me now "I asked repeatedly without any answer, I lay on her bed and covered myself with her duvet just so I just smell her, I missed her scent, I clutched her pillow between my arms and I filled it with my tears and I cried until I could cry no more. I walked back into my room and I lay there wondering what my life would be like without my mother. The next morning I woke up as usual and jumped out of my bed and walked straight to my mother's to go and kiss her and say good morning, as I entered the room a cold breeze hit me and for a second I stood in shock and instantly I had a flashbacks of what had happened the night before, my mother wasn't in her room, she would never be in her room again because she was dead and in that very moment as I stood in that cold room my ears suddenly popped and I heard the cries downstairs, I sat on the floor and gathered my thoughts and in that moment I wished that it was all a dream.

The process to the funeral was distressing, everyone came with their opinions and everyone believed they knew what was best for her and the truth was that a lot of these people were fakes, fake family and fake friends; they came and cried with us at home and went back and secretly rejoiced because that is who they were. My mother never realised that she didn't have genuine friends, she had people that she helped so much and those same people became the cause of her downfall, a lesson that I learned very early on. Family came from America and from other cities in the UK for her burial, arrangements were made and we prepared to say goodbye to our mother. The funeral came by and just like that, the entire process was painful and tiring; our house was full of family and friends everyday so things didn't really settle into our minds about what was about to happen to us. Our mother was buried the Muslim way because she was born as a Muslim, I remember crying and screaming so much that I had to be locked in the car and held down by my best friend Leah. It was hard for me to come to terms with not being able to see my mother again, the worst part was driving away from the cemetery and thinking about her alone in that place with no one around her and that broke me. Being the youngest I was babied a lot by my aunts and cousins who did anything to make me smile, some would take me shopping and others would just sit with me and tell me funny stories and buy me food. Some of my aunts who came from America arranged with my siblings for me to go to the states to spend some time with them and return before our mothers 40th day Muslim ceremony. I went to the states and had a great time meeting my extended family and friends, I got to meet Aunty Binty, who was my mother's dearest friend, I had heard so many stories about her and she seemed unreal until I met her and understood exactly why my mother cherished her so much. She made the process of my healing better because she nurtured me so much during that time and told me great stories about my mother.

Returning back from the states was a reality check, the 40th day ceremony was now over and everyone left and then we had to deal with the emptiness. Rakie took the lead as the head of the family as best as she could and for the first few months things were fine, we tried to readjust our lives to living without our mother and made the relevant changes. The aunties and uncles that promised to keep in touch and look after us called for the first few months and then everyone just went silent and went back to their normal lives because after all it wasn't their burden to carry. Lamin and Rashida went back to work and so did Abdul, Me and Rakie were alone in the house trying to make sense of our lives. I was in my last year of college and I was doing well but after my mother passed I knew the pressure had mounted. Rakie had conversations with me often telling me that I needed to work hard because our mother wasn't here anymore and all we had was each other. She had to leave university and start working full-time in order to pay the bills at home, she worked mostly nights and I went to college; the first few months of college was fine, I was so focused on getting my grades so that I would be able to get into university because I wanted to go to London. I started isolating myself from my friends and stopped going out, I wasn't eating or sleeping properly and my weight was dropping severely. Most days after college I would go to my mother's grave and just cry, I would cry to the point where my head would start spinning. I started going to her grave four times a week that was the only place where I felt okay; being near her and being able to feel like she was still a part of my life because I didn't want to let her go. I would cry myself to sleep most nights, I was in agony and I wondered if I would ever be able to stop crying because people said that after a while the crying would stop but mine only seemed to get worse. I only ate because my stomach would hurt but rarely did I feel hungry, I started buying boys t-shirts and jeans and I would wear them to college with those big bumper jackets to try and conceal my extreme weight loss. My body had drained and I did everything possible to try and put the weight back on but it wasn't happening.

One day I was home cleaning the kitchen, I was wiping the table because there was this stain that was stubborn and wouldn't wipe away so I kept wiping, I used soap and then bleach and it still wasn't going so I started crying and found a scrubber because I wanted that stain to go. I needed that table to be clean and in that process Rakie walked in and screamed my name and when I looked up at her she said " Fatmata this is not your portion, you are not going to be frustrated " I started crying and she hugged me and started praying for me, we had a long conversation and she told me that she has noticed my weight loss and how I have become very withdrawn from my friends and that I spend a lot of time at home and that's not like me. I had no explanation to give but I promised to make an effort to take better care of myself. That same week my tutors at college called me for a meeting and they expressed that they were concerned about me;

they said although my grades are good and I was doing well academically they had noticed a change in how I dressed and how I relate with my peers, they concluded that I was depressed and struggling to deal with the loss of my mother and with that they set me up for in-college counselling and extra tutor support. I was so grateful for them because they became my family and always made sure that I was okay. Rakie started encouraging me to go to church with her as she believed it would help me with my healing as she stated that God was her only source of strength and seeing was believing because for years we had prayed together at home and attended some churches in Manchester but I had never really had a church to cal home or given my life to Christ. I visited Rakie's church and the people were nice, they were supportive and really understood what we were going through and always prayed with us. On one particular Sunday I remember so clearly how down I had been feeling that week and when we went to church on Sunday the message was exactly what I needed to hear, it gave me hope; it was about not giving up regardless of how bad things may seem or how heavy your heart may feel. The pastor did an alter call for whoever wanted to give their life to Jesus and for the first time I felt so connected, for the past year I had been in agony dealing with the loss of my mother and making sense of who I was now and what my life would be without her. I stood up and went to the front and as the Pastor lay his hands on me and prayed I felt a relief, a weight being lifted as tears started to roll down my cheeks, it felt like I was being comforted spiritually; something inside of me changed that day and I became hopeful again. When I stood up there I believed that God saw me, he saw all my pain and all the tears that I had been crying and I envisioned that he stood before me with his arms wide open and without knowing or planning or even understanding there I was knocking on heaven's door.

7 LAUGHING THROUGH THE PAIN

I was accepted into all my choices for
university and I was so ecstatic and ready for
what would be a great new chapter in my life,
my siblings were all so proud of me and I had
made the decision that I would study at London
Metropolitan University. I left college with a
great record, student of the year for business
and professional studies for two years in a row
and I also received a £1000 scholarship from
Baroness Helena Kennedy towards my
university studies. The time came for me to
leave came and my siblings rallied around to
send me off, Lamin, Abdul and Rakie all packed
with me and we drove to London to my student
accommodation which was in Tufnell Park in
North London. I couldn't believe that this was
actually my life, for the first time in my life I
started to see the fruitfulness of my hard work
and I was proud of myself. I hugged Rakie so
tightly and I cried as I said goodbye to them,
Abdul prayed for me and Lamin told me some
jokes to lift my spirit up. I think I was prepared
and ready to face my adult life, I had enough
experience of budgeting during the times when

things were so bad for me and Rakie that we lived on a weekly £20 food budget because all the other money had to go towards the bills and we were alone. Rakie taught me how to make meals on a £5 budget and our mother had taught us the importance of buying extra food and clothes for those rainy days. I was ready for university, I was ready to meet new people and make my own decisions on what I thought was best for me; well I thought I was ready but life has a way of reminding you that you are never truly in control of your own life.

On the first student mixer night I got to meet some of the girls that lived in my halls, I was on the ground floor so I instantly built friendships with my neighbors who were Sara who was a beautiful Caucasian girl from Halifax, Fatima who was a Sudanese girl from Nottingham and Sayaka who was an intentional student from Japan. I was blessed to have met a group of such amazing women who gave me so much insight into their cultural backgrounds; we ate each other's foods and partied together. I found a new family while I was away from home and that was so comforting, Fatima and I were the closest in the group; we seemed to gel more and understood each other's humor so much that sometimes we finished each other's sentences. We cooked together most evenings and we would sit down and laugh at the funny things that happened to us on campus. For those first few months I forgot about my struggles, pain and worries and I was just being myself, a young girl with no worries except the thought of having to write those three thousand word essays. I was studying HRM which Rakie said was a great industry to get into. During one of my management classes I met a girl who would later become more of my lifelong friends and her name was Tadeyo. I can't remember how we started talking but I know that the second we met we just glued together, we bonded over our love for the American dream and the fact that we were the only girls on campus that owned sidekick phones. So we exchanged sidekick details and that was the beginning of a beautiful friendship. I made a lot of friends at London met and I had a lot of fun, it was so good meeting likeminded people, I was living the London dream.

I got to go to the best clubs and parties and wear the best of what I wanted, I was carefree but as time went on reality started to settle in with me.

Not Easily Broken

While I was at university My father found a
way to get into contact with me, a part of me
was so ecstatic and wanted so badly to get
reconnected and have him back in my life since
my mother was no longer around but another
part of me was angry. I knew that he didn't
have a way of remaining in contact with me
because he was serving his time but I was still
angry because he wasn't there for me when I
needed him. I needed my father to comfort me
when I lost my mother and he wasn't there. Our
first few conversations were good, he told me
about what life has been like for him and how
much he loved me and missed me and he was
so proud of me for being able to cope by
myself. He asked me when I would be going
back to Sierra Leone and I told him that it
would need to be after I finished my first year
of university so that I would have a clearer
idea of my schedule. I went Manchester some
weekends to reconnect with my friends, I was
home sick but I didn't realise it until I started
going back home; I don't know whether it was
the visits back to Manchester but after my first
year of university things didn't go so well for
me. I lost all interest in the course I was
studying and we received news that my
grandmother mama Fatu who was my mother's

mother had passed away. Her death hit me
hard because it felt personal to me especially
after I was told that she struggled to deal with
my mother's death. My aunty Zainabu told me
that my grandmother died of a broken heart;
she said that my grandmother was never the
same after my mother's death. Things were
tough for me in London, financially I did my
best to keep my head above water but there
were times when I struggled to pay my housing
rent and just exist. I had family in London but
as much as everyone told me that I could ask
them for help it wasn't an easy thing for me to
do. My friends helped me out a few times when
I was really in a bad space and at that time I
started to rethink whether or not university
was the best place for me because I was still
struggling emotionally and I wasn't making the
right decisions. I realised that I always acted
out of impulse because of the feeling of control
that I got from those moments. I liked the idea
of the things that I was doing but the choices
that I made were taking me to places I wasn't
meant to be. I left university and packed my
belongings and returned back to Manchester, I
wasn't sure whether studying was something
that I even wanted to do ever again; I just
knew that I wasn't passionate about studying or

even working in human resources.

Once I was back in Manchester I didn't know what I wanted to do with my life but I knew that I needed to take care of myself, I had good work experience and references so I went back into waitressing and started making some good money from that. It wasn't the easiest of jobs but I did make good tips and through that I was able to make up my mind about going back home to Sierra Leone to see my father. One of my friends Kai was going to Sierra Leone for the Christmas holiday and told me to come along and even offered me a place to stay at his family house. I worked really hard and booked my ticket and prepared myself for the journey back home. It was December 2009 and I was super excited to be going back home, it was a little bitter sweet because I knew that at the back of my mind returning home meant that old wounds may be opened up and I wasn't sure how much blood would pour out. I was so excited when I was checking in at the airport, I was excited to see my dad and all my family, I hadn't seen them in over ten years and I knew that a lot had changed. I landed at Lungi international airport and that breeze that hit me as soon as I walked down those aeroplane

stairs was the best feeling in the world. I loved
seeing those green trees and the chaos that
was inside the airport, I knew I was home.
While I was collecting my luggage one of my
cousins that worked at the airport saw me and
called my father and told him that I had come
to Sierra Leone, I was extremely angry
because my months of planning was all ruined
because of a mouthy family member. He
walked over to me and gave me his mobile and
told me my father was on the phone, I took the
phone rolling my eyes at him and there on the
other line was my father full of joy and asked
me why I didn't tell him that I was coming and I
told him that I wanted to surprise him. My
friend Kai picked me up from the airport and
we went straight to my father's house and on
my arrival everything was different because
the rebels had burnt down our house but my
father had started building another house at the
back of the land which is where they now lived.
It was dark because it was after 9pm, so I
walked into the house and just like when I was
five when they first took me to Sierra Leone
everyone started shouting my name and
hugging me but I was only concerned with one
person and that was my father, I saw him and
grabbed him into a hug and we both started

crying. It was the best feeling in the world, it was like we were never apart; I was daddy's girl again and my heart was at peace in that particular moment.

I met some of my extended family members; my sisters were there and so was my brother Borboh (number 1). My step-mothers were present but looked like different versions of themselves; it's amazing what a lack of money can do to certain people. I spent some time catching up with my father and family but told them I had to leave because we had a far distance to travel, I promised my dad that I would call him and we would make arrangements to meet the following day and then I left. I sat in the car on the journey to Kai's house and enjoyed the view, Freetown wasn't the same anymore but no one could steal away the beauty of my country in my eyes. No matter how damaged the roads looked or the lack of electricity there was still something so beautiful about Sierra Leone and I was ready to explore again. I had such a great time in Freetown, I was able to meet other Sierra Leonean's that were on holiday and that made my trip more fun. I did a lot of clubbing and spent a lot of time at the beach,

My father told me how important it was for me to come home often and reminded me that I had a family there and he wanted to make up for all the time he missed while I was growing up. I was resentful and I told him that I felt as though he didn't do as much for me as he did for his other children, I didn't get his time or his money because my mother did everything for me. He found it difficult to talk about my mother's death, he would start speaking about it and then something inside of him would get heavy and he would just shake his head and end the conversation and in those moments I still saw the look of love in my father's eyes. For the first time everything made sense and I realised why my bond with my father was different and why so many people thought I was his favorite, it wasn't actually about me; it was about my mother, the woman he loved and I was the product of their love. I made the decision to forgive him and start working on rebuilding whatever I believed had been lost or broken, I spent a lot of time with him during my holiday and made myself a promise that no matter what it took I needed to come home every year to see my father, I had already lost my mother and he was all I had left and I needed to cherish him and make up for the mistakes I made with my mother.

I returned back to Manchester and continued to work, I started working in the social care sector; it was a better job with better pay and career development so it was a good move to make until I decided what I wanted to do next. I worked really hard and was looking forward to my next trip to Sierra Leone, the time came and I went back again this time I stayed with my Uncle Francis my father's younger brother. Again my trip was eventful, I spent a lot of time with friends that were also on holiday and people I met on my travels but the most eventful part of my holiday was meeting Daddy K. His name was Abdul, he had the same name as my brother; He was dark skinned, medium height and had long thick dreads. We met on the flight coming to Sierra Leone when we were delayed for an entire day and spent the night at a hotel in Heathrow which the airline paid for. He kept looking at me and tried so hard to get my attention but I ignored him because he seemed so over confident and I didn't like that. When we got to Lungi airport and we were collecting our luggage, he came over to me and said hi, I said hi back and turned away, he flirted with me and told me

177

jokes and I laughed but I ignored him because I could tell he was so use to getting his way with women because he was a smooth talker. He was with his brother and friends and they seemed so agitated by him spending so much time trying to pursue me, he asked me for my contact details and I declined telling him that he was a stranger and then he said "I can tell that your stubborn but trust me we will meet again and you will be my girlfriend ", I laughed because I admired his confidence and I walked away still laughing and I went to catch the ferry with my friends that I met on the flight. That same night I went home had a shower and straight away I was out the house with my cousins to go to Paddy's which was the place to be in those days, I looked good that night so I walked and talked like I knew I was the deal. As I was walking past the bar someone grabbed my hand and when I turned around it was him and he smiled and said "I told you we would meet again "I laughed because this time there was something about his eyes that caught me off guard, he spoke to me for a little while and told me he knew I had a Sierra Leone number now and asked me for it, I told him no and he told me that If I didn't give him my number his brother and friends would laugh at him because his been trying to talk to me since we were in London and I kept making him look desperate by ignoring him. I looked across the room and there they all were staring at us talk and I chuckled a little and asked him why he was so adamant about me. He smiled and said that he didn't know but he had a very strong feeling that I was going to be his girlfriend, and my heart started beating so fast and then for the first time I realised that I liked men that were confident and were able to cater to my need to be stubborn at times and are willing to fight for my attention. I gave him my cousin's number, he was so happy and he told me he would call me to take me out on a date I said okay and I left. He called the next day but I let him stew for a few days before getting back to him and I purposely avoided going to Paddy's in case I saw him. When I called him back he told me that he was the captain of the game that I was trying to play but he would let my behavior slide because he liked me and we both laughed. He came and picked me up in his Chrysler 300c dressed all in white with his long thick dreads and he smelt like tropical fruits and looked like he tasted like honey, Abdul was fine in my eyes because confidence is what turned me on.

On our first date he took out a picture from his wallet and showed me his son that he had from his previous relationship and even told me about his son's mother. Abdul lived in New York at the time and was doing diamond mining in Sierra Leone and Guinea. He was so open and honest with me that I was afraid, I was twenty and he was twenty five, I had only been in one relationship before meeting Abdul and I actually thought that our relationship was only Sierra Leone bound because of the distance and knowing and seeing the type of guy he was I didn't think it would work. He was hot stuff, he was a hot pick, I was young and inexperienced and I didn't think I had what he needed because I was still maturing but he was sure and he wanted to see where things would go so we decided to be in relationship. I returned to Manchester and he returned to the states, we talked like twice a day but he travelled to Sierra Leone a lot. Abdul was so attentive and open with me all the time, he was like a father and boyfriend all rolled into one. He would always kiss and cuddle me and taught me a lot of the things I now know about relationships. I was so ashamed of my body and being intimate with men because of my past which I told him about and everyday he would tell that I was so beautiful and that my body belonged to me and not the man that did what he did to me. I fell head over hills in love with him to the point where I felt sick at times if we had an argument and didn't talk for two days. He would always sing Collie Budz "Tomorrow's another day "to me and would tell me that I had so many emotional issues that I needed to deal with because it was affecting our relationship. He was still insisting that he loved me and wanted to make it work. We tried our best to make it work, He bought me a ticket and I went to the states to see him and he met my cousins who loved him; he would come and pick me up and take me to dinner and we would have long talks about our future. Abdul was a practicing Muslim and I was a Christian so I was often conflicted about having to convert if we got married and that was something I told him I couldn't do and he told me that was fine, he said we could be married and both following the faiths we wanted but I didn't like the idea of having different religious beliefs and I always expressed that to him but he was always so nonchalant about it all.

A few months after I returned to the UK Abdul was in Guinea on business and we spoke often while he was travelling except he was somewhere that there was no network. He called one particular night and he was drunk, I could hear women in the background and without realising he told me that he wanted to break up because he didn't think that he was committed, he spoke about how loyal I was and how young I was and stated that being with me made him feel like he wasn't good enough to me because I was basically too good to be true in other words. I cried myself to sleep that night because I didn't understand what had happened; my relationship with Abdul at the time was the only good thing in my life that I was sure about. He called me the next day and tried to pretend that he didn't remember what happened but I jogged his memory and we had a heart to heart and he was honest that the temptation was a lot for him and he didn't want to cheat on me and have to lie to me because he loved me. I cried on the phone, he said he wasn't ready but he wasn't closing our chapter and I told him that if he goes that was it for me because I couldn't leave my heart on the line until he was ready and just like that Abdul broke my heart without warning, what was laughter quickly turned to pain. I cried for a while, every time I would think about him I would cry because I had really fallen for him and I started to picture our life together. I was due to go to Sierra Leone in the next few months so I decided to heal my heart and show him that I was okay without him because I knew he would be in Sierra Leone that December.

I went to Sierra Leone for the third time and I was looking good, fresh out of a relationship and my heart was almost healed. I enjoyed myself so much and danced away all of the pain when I would go out clubbing with my cousins, I didn't see Abdul when I went out so I knew that he was still in Guinea. One night my cousins and I went to watch the Miss Paddy's beauty pageant at Paddy's night club and there I saw some of my male cousins from the states. I went over to say hi and I had these extremely high heels on and they were burning my feet so I asked one of my cousins to carry me to the other side of the club because I couldn't walk on the stones. My cousin said that he couldn't but pointed to this tall handsome guy with an amazing body and a beautiful smile and said that he would carry me. He lifted me up and took me to the flat ground and put me down and we both laughed, he introduced himself to me and I must say there was no denying it he was fine and my hormones were running wild. We talked for a little while and he asked me for my number, I didn't hesitate so I gave it to him and he said that he would call me. His name was Didi, he also lived in the states; my cousins asked me if I was cursed for American men and I told them that I had a radar. Me and Didi started communicating via text and he invited me to go to Kono with him, Kono is another city in Sierra Leone, the city where my father and his family are from, I told him that I couldn't go because my father would not allow me to travel and he begged me to find a way and to meet him there. Luckily my cousin was scheduled to travel to Kono at the time so I used her as an excuse for my Dad to allow me to go. I went to Kono to meet him and that was the start of our story, Didi made me shy, there was a connection between us that I couldn't really understand but I liked him. We started spending time together during the holiday, I met some of his family and he did mine and most nights we went clubbing and we would spend the night together. One night me and my girls were at Paddy's and Didi was also there with his boys, we were having fun and enjoying the vibe and the music and as I walked across the bar there he was, his eyes caught mine and I was in total shock. Abdul ran over to me and told me how happy he was to see me, he said that his been looking for me everywhere, he didn't even care that he was speaking loudly, he was pouring his heart out and telling me how much he missed me and that he made a big mistake and he was ready to make that wrong right. I stood in a frozen position shocked and trying to digest what he was telling me, His brother came over and angrily told him to man up and stop acting like a pussy and his reply was "I love her "and that was it for me, My heart fell and instantly I was confused and in that moment my friend Abie whispered to me "Didi is over there looking I think we should walk away ". We tried to walk away and Abdul grabbed me and I whispered to him that I couldn't talk now and he asked me why and I told him because I was dating someone else and he was there and I didn't want to disrespect him and Abdul's face froze and I quickly made an escape with my friend Abie.

Didi didn't look happy so I walked over to him and pulled him into a hug to give him assurance and straight away he asked me who the guy was that was trying to talk to me and I told him that he was the ex I told him about and he looked at me in shock and said "That's your ex "and I said yes and it turned out that they knew of each other but didn't know each other. Me and Didi left and went home but a few nights later we had another incident at another night club with Abdul and this time him and Didi came face to face when Abdul told me that he was willing to do whatever it took to get me back and even told me he was ready to go and see my father and ask for my hand in marriage. I told him that I was with Didi now and he had already decided that he wasn't ready and I wasn't going to end things with Didi just because he wanted me back, he begged me to give him another chance and started talking about our past and our good memories and honestly I wanted to say yes and make it work again but I couldn't trust him that he was sure about me. He had broken my heart and left me for months without caring about how I was doing or if I was okay. I liked what I was building with Didi and It was new and refreshing and I wanted to see how far we could go because I liked Didi and just like Abdul I liked his confidence and his ambition and how he made me feel. I had a decision to make and I did what was right in that moment and I told Abdul that I was sticking with Didi because I liked him and with a sorrowful heart his last words to me were "I hope you know what you're doing because the devil you know is better than the angel you don't know "and just like that our chapter came to an end.

There was a big part of me that was sad because I never wanted him out of my life fully, I always thought that we would have some type of relationship even if our love relationship never worked but Abdul was the proud type, he was a Gemini and pride is their national anthem. The decision was less about Didi and more about me and how I felt at that time, the trust was gone, I was afraid of giving him my heart again because I had loved him so deeply and he broke my heart I couldn't give him a second chance to do it again. I focused on just enjoying my holiday and trying to make the most of whatever it was that was happening between me and Didi, just like it started with Abdul it was suppose to be a holiday romance with Didi too but we both caught feelings and decide to take our relationship outside the shores of Sierra Leone. We were young and I think we both fell for each other hard, I thought

that what I felt for Abdul was love until my
chapter with Didi started to unravel, only then
did I realise what it really meant to be in love
and the extents that love can push you too.

8 THE TEST AND THE TESTIMONY

It was 2011 and I was back at university
studying for the second time round, I was in a
relationship with Didi and things seemed okay.
Rakie was now married and had left me at the
house and went to live with her husband. My
life was like a rollercoaster; it would go really
high up and quickly come back down. I was
studying in Crewe which was an hour away
from Manchester, I enrolled on a creative
writing course and I thought at this time I
would pursue my dream of becoming a writer
because writing was the one thing that I felt
that I did effortlessly. I still had my part time
job and mostly worked occasional weekends
when work was available, my siblings checked
in with me once in a while as and when they
felt or if I called them. I, Abdul and Rakie
attended the same church so I saw them most
Sundays and sometimes Abdul would pick me

up and take me to church which I appreciated. I had a strong bond with my mother's dearest friend Aunty Binty and I would spend most of my holidays in the states with her and her children. Edward Aunty Binty's son or my eddy weddy as I named him was a chef, he is funny and kind and so full of life and laughter, he would always call me and say "Fatmata when are you coming to America to cook cassava leaf, that's the only reason I want you to come for the cassava leaf and the mar bars from London ". Elizabeth my Lizzy as I call her, she is strong, independent and so full of life and is never apologetic for her choices and I love her for that. They never realised just how much they helped me through my mother's death, their love, support and kindness is what helped to heal the wounds in my heart. Me and Aunty Binty would sit down for hours and just talk about my mother and their younger days and she spent a lot of time advising me about life. While I was dating Didi it was great to be able to spend time with him while I was in the states.

Before I travelled to the states I received information that Didi was still seeing his ex girlfriend, I was devastated because I thought that he was different. I did so much and invested so much to make the relationship work but it just seemed like he just kept wrapping me up in his lies. I was in love and so far gone that even when I saw the open lies I chose to take the words from his lips as my truth and in that I wrapped myself in my own web of deceit. By the time I got to America we were already on non-speaking terms and Tadeyo warned me to not fall under his spell again because we had travelled to the states together. The day after I arrived I got a call from Didi asking if he could come and see me and at first I said no because I wanted to stick to what I had told my friends that I wouldn't do but after he said he just wanted to talk. In the end I gave in because deep down inside I missed him and I wanted to see him so he came over and we sat down and talked. We talked about the issues we were having the lies he insisted he didn't tell and before I could say wait a minute I was back under his spell so I had to gently break the news to my friends and being who they were they just told me to be careful and don't jump back in fully. We spent most of the holiday together and everything was fine, it was my birthday and Didi wanted me to spend the weekend with him in New

Jersey. I told Aunty Binty, packed my weekend bag and he picked me up. He was in a very petty mood and spent a lot of the journey telling me that I do too much and I didn't need to dress up all the time and he wanted me to sometimes just be like an average girl that didn't need to be all done up to go out. As he spoke my heart fell and I started thinking about Abdul, he was the opposite; he never degraded me or said anything to break my self-esteem but I took it because maybe this was an issue that needed to be addressed. We got to the hotel and we checked in and went to our room, he asked me to write a thank you message for him on his computer that he needed to post on facebook for all the people that had attended a P-Square concert that he and his partner had organised. Didi fell asleep and I sat on the laptop and as I typed I became curious and wondered what I would find if I looked in his facebook inbox. I decided to follow my instincts and I typed the name of his ex girlfriend and their conversation came up and I saw evidence up to a few days before that he was still communicating with her and telling her all types of love stories. As I finished reading the messages he jumped out of his sleep as if he knew what I was doing and rushed across the bed and snatched the laptop out of my hand but it was too late. He saw that I had seen the messages and he got angry and started screaming and telling me that I was wrong and stupid. He got dressed and he left the room, he didn't come back until 3am in the morning. When he returned he woke me up by making calls to girls he was either dating or ex girlfriends but I was shocked, I lay on my bed and cried silent tears as I was forced to listen to his conversations and I saw a side to this man that I didn't know existed. The next morning we woke up and he got ready and left me in the room and went to have breakfast, I had a shower and went downstairs and there he was sitting by himself eating breakfast. I got myself some food and sat down opposite him and ate my food and he got up and left. I was feeling so low because he refused to speak to me and wanted to turn the fact that I caught him in a lie on me. I couldn't finish my breakfast so I went upstairs and realised that he had left me in the hotel alone and gone out so I started calling some friends to ask them to come and rescue me but I was too far away and the hotel we were at was in an awkward area. I didn't bring any money with me and I didn't want to inconvenience my aunty or even tell her what was happening so she wouldn't worry so I just tried to handle the situation. I started feeling dizzy so I went to lay down but I didn't feel better, I thought that it was probably the stress so I kept drinking water because that was all that there was and I didn't have any money to buy food. I felt wetness in my panties so I went into the bathroom and saw that I was bleeding but it wasn't period blood so I called one of my friends and told her what was going on. The nearest hospital was an hour away and ambulances cost $900 in America so I had no choice but to self heal. I changed my underwear but I continued to bleed so I went online and did some research and I also called one of my friends that was a medical professional because at this point I was so distressed and she told me that I was miscarrying. I didn't know what to feel or to think so I just ended the call and went to lie down on the bed and cried myself a river as I bleed away. He left me alone in that hotel from Friday evening until Sunday morning when we were leaving, he had no idea what I had gone through over that weekend and he was angry because I caught him in a lie. The drive back was silent and once we got back I asked him to just drop me at the end of my aunt's road and I

got out slammed the door and I walked to the
house crying. There was nobody home so I
went into the shower and lay my body naked in
the bathroom and I cried so bitterly and I
prayed for God to grant me strength because I
felt like he had taken so much away from me,
my peace, my respect, my dignity and even the
life of a child that I didn't even know was
there. I started grieving for a loss that I didn't
understand, I was so angry with him and I
realised that he could never be the man that I
needed him to be. For me it was not the same
after that, that relationship ended on the basis
of physical abuse, a few months later we got
into a fight in Sierra Leone and he beat me and
ripped the weave-on from my head and I was
stripped naked and left with a swollen body. He
then ended the relationship and openly and
proudly started parading a new relationship
that he was already in while we were together.

I was devastated; I started to think that there
was something wrong with me. I became
insecure and I was broken all over again, he
was so wicked to me for someone that I had
loved so much and supported so much, it was
hard to accept that he wasn't who I thought he
was. While I was in the states I received a

message from my mother's sister Aunty B who I had been searching for since she passed away. I was so happy and couldn't wait to get to know her, I told my siblings about her contacting me and they were not happy and told me that they were not interested in building a relationship with her. I was actually sad to hear them say that but I didn't care because I was ready and willing to know her, some of my siblings even threatened me that if I pursued the relationship with her they would have less to do with me. It came across like a big joke to me because they had all abandoned me and they wanted me to not speak to the only other family that I had in the UK just because they felt salty. I ignored their opinions and connected with my Aunty, she sounded exactly like my mother and was so full or joy and laughter; it was like having my mother back at times. Aunty B invited me to go to London to meet her and her family and I was happy, they booked me a travel ticket and they went to meet me at the station, when she saw me she cried and hugged me so tightly and I cried because I saw so much of my mother in her it was painful. My Aunty had six children and lived with her husband Uncle John in Hackney, when I got to the house I met everyone and instantly I felt the love. They were all so unified and they were kind to me and did whatever it took to make me comfortable, Aunty B and Uncle John made sure she got my hair done for me and bought me anything that I needed while I was with them. We had a chance to speak about the issues between her and my mother and she explained her side of the story because for many years the Sierra Leonean community painted the picture that they wanted and that is what they sold. For a long time I had been struggling in Manchester with no support from my siblings, everyone was living their own lives and they didn't care about what I needed. I was 22 years old and living alone not understanding or ever being taught about bills and responsibility, I am so thankful for Alex Kabia and My Aunty B who were the people who saved me from my sorrows during those times. Sometimes things were so tight for me financially that I wouldn't have food to eat and I would have to call Alex and tell him what was going on and he would bring me some money to buy food. I remember sending one of my siblings a text message one day and begged them for £10 so I could buy electricity for the house because it was on emergency credit and

they texted me back saying that they didn't
have any money. I cried and cried and
wondered what I had ever done to offend them
because they had truly turned their backs on
me. One of my friends in church Shirley who
was Ghanaian would often walk with me after
church on Sundays and one Sunday I confided
in her that I actually didn't have any money or
food at home at the time and she was shocked
and amazed and asked me about my siblings
and I told her when I ask them they say they
don't have money. Shirley took me to the
supermarket and bought me enough food to
last me the week and gave me some cash and
told me to never be ashamed to speak to her if
things got this bad again. I cried and I thanked
her and every day I just prayed that God would
pull me out of whatever it was that I was going
through.

I remember a particular Sunday when I saw my
siblings in church and after service I heard
them saying they were going to eat Chinese so
I walked over and spoke to them and asked
them if I could come along with them and they
made an excuse that they had someone to go
and visit and they left. Every week I would
hear stories in Church about the outings that

my siblings would have with other church members, inviting them to dinners and activities, It was so painful to hear that my own blood siblings were treating me like I was a homeless dog that they didn't want to be near but I still tried to not take it to heart. I did my best to survive and started to realise that I couldn't cope because I couldn't pay the rent, I couldn't feed myself and with that my grades were falling in university so with that I left again because I couldn't focus and I just concluded that something or someone somewhere didn't want me to get my degree so I gave up and there was no one to encourage me to keep going. I had a friend called Amy who was Sierra Leonean and lived in London, she was aware of everything that I was going through and told me to come back to London and start my life again. I thought about it and realised that there was nothing left for me in Manchester at least in London I would be able to start afresh and rebuild my life. I called all my siblings and told them that I was giving up the house because it was in arrears and I couldn't afford to pay the rent, no one really cared so without thinking twice or looking back I packed my belongings and I left. I sold whatever I could in the house which wasn't

more than £500 and I used that to keep myself
fed for the first month in London. I moved in
with Amy and I was able to continuing working
with the same company that I had worked with
in Manchester in London as an agency staff. I
used that Job as my way of survival, I lived
with Amy but then I lived with other people
too. I started making some of the wrong friends
in the Sierra Leonean community and just like
that I was jumping from one friend to another
from one house to another. The people that I
thought were my friends and we all seemed to
have the same struggle were the worse, I
realised that I couldn't trust any of them
because whatever help them gave was so that
they could have information to spread about
me. A lot of these people seemed like they
were nice but they were full of drama and
chaos, they loved knowing and being in other
people's business. It took me a while to learn
but moving to London and being around Sierra
Leonean people taught me the toughest lessons
in the quickest time. I was still connected to
Tadeyo and we continued to build our
friendship and during this time I was still
dealing with the drama of Didi who seemed to
always have something negative to say about
me even though we were no longer together

and this really affected me emotionally. people used me and abused my kindness so much that I almost forgot my value and forgot who I was, I was dealing with so many things spiritually and emotionally that I fell into many traps and made many mistakes that I regret today; I learnt that Pain will take you to places that you never thought you would reach if you don't deal with it before it deals with you. I still made sure that in the midst of all of this I was still trying to support my father financially and kept my promise to visit him every year in Sierra Leone, maybe that wasn't the best decision for me but who was around that could fully advice me.

In 2012 I went to Sierra Leone for three months to start my charity project which was focused on working with mothers and babies, during those three months I met someone that I thought was genuine to me, when I look back at it now I understand clearly that I was in no way emotionally stable and he knew that. At the time he seemed nice and genuine and said all the right things but I never had feelings for him and I told him that. My friends encouraged me to give him a chance because he liked me and sometimes it's better to be with someone who

loves you more than you love them but the
reality was that I didn't love him. I looked back
at my previous relationship and I told myself
that I loved those men and they broke my trust
and broke my heart so maybe the advice they
were giving was right, I should give him a
chance just because he liked me and he was a
nice guy. So I gave him a chance and we
started dating, he was doing everything right
and I was doing everything to try and make it
work because maybe I was getting
relationships wrong all along, maybe the key
was to force yourself to be in a relationship
with someone you didn't love just because they
loved you. I really tried to love him but the
more I was with him the more I realised I was
living a lie and I just didn't want to be in a
loveless relationship with someone I didn't see
a future with. In my mind I was ready to end
the relationship and told myself that I would it
do it just before I returned back to the UK. I
had my plans but God knew something different
was coming, In September 2012 I discovered
that I was pregnant in the most unlikely way
possible, I was shocked and afraid and
disappointed, I wasn't ready but I told God that
I would cherish the next child he gave me and I
refused to break that promise. I wasn't sad

about the pregnancy but I was sad about the person I was pregnant for because now we were bonded for life, I didn't love him so I started wondering if I would love my baby, all types of questions came to mind because fear started to set in. I begged my father to quickly book me a return ticket back to the UK which he did and I flew back immediately because I didn't feel safe being pregnant and being in Sierra Leone. The flight back to the UK was one of the longest flights I have ever been on; it was the same seven hours as I always travelled but the confusion in my mind made everything more intense. The hardest part was having to accept that now I needed to stay in a relationship that I didn't want because I was too ashamed of how people would judge me, I was more concerned about what the church folks would say, Christian girl pregnant and not married; I was so afraid.

I kept my pregnancy under wraps for the first five months as I prepared to become a mother. I was homeless at the time and waiting to be housed by the government in which time I went to stay with a friend who was living with her son and invited me to stay with them until my housing was in place, this was a decision that I would later regret. My pregnancy wasn't the most pleasant because I spent a lot of my time in hospital, I had hyperemesis gravidarum and this made my pregnancy more difficult because I spent most of my time vomiting and I could hardly eat anything without throwing it back up. I was stressed and worried and in an emotionally abusive relationship, my child's father was so possessive and manipulating that he always had his ways of try to control my emotions or actions; when I thought about the fact that I would have to deal with him for the rest of my life I would feel so down. I was still working to save money to be able to buy what I needed for the baby, I worked mostly night jobs as it was easier for me to complete my forty hours in a few days. My daughter's father would call me while I was at work heavily pregnant and start accusing me of cheating and making up stories of hearing a man's voice in the background, he was so horrible to me and a part of me just wished I could end the relationship and focus on raising my child alone but whenever I thought about my father my heart would sink and I would convince myself that staying with my daughters father was the best decision.

On March 30th 2013 I was at my friends house
hanging out with some group of people when I
received a phone call from Sierra Leone, My
sister Hawa was on the phone crying and I
asked her what was wrong and she said
"Fatmata Daddy is dead ", the phone fell out of
my hand and my knees went weak and I felt my
body collapsing to the floor when my friends
rushed to catch me as I screamed and cried.
That was it, the worst day of my life, the day
that I prayed and prayed for God not to allow
had finally come and there I was helpless. I
cried uncontrollable and everyone was trying
to comfort me but reminding me that I was
pregnant and needed to think about the baby. I
was seven months pregnant and I hadn't gotten
the chance to tell my father, I was waiting for
the right time and in that moment I just wished
that I would have told him; maybe knowing I
was about to have a baby would have made a
difference. The news spread quickly and
people started to call me but I didn't want to
talk to anyone I just wanted my father back. I
wanted to see him and feel him and hold his
body before it was cold, I sat down in silence
as I tried to understand what was happening in
my life, everything I was doing was to make
him proud; I was existing because he gave me

hope and now he was gone and I couldn't understand it at all. My child's father called and tried to console me and in that same sentence advised me not to travel to Sierra Leone for my father's burial because it wasn't safe for the baby. Everyone said the same thing and the more people spoke I became angrier because they didn't understand the pain and rage I was feeling, how could anyone ask me to not pay my last respect to my father, did they know the bond that we shared and what I was feeling. I did everything I could to raise enough money for me to travel to Sierra Leone. My child's father called me selfish and said that I was putting our child's life at risk and told me to send him whatever money I had so that he could represent me at my father's funeral. I couldn't blame him because he didn't have a relationship with his father like I did with mine so he couldn't possibly understand what I was feeling that was why he could easily dismiss my pain and suggest something so classless.

I went all the way to my father's village and even sat in the car with his coffin and I cried all the way knowing that this was the end of the road. My heart ached when they lay him down in the ground; it felt like I was reliving the loss of my mother all over again. I couldn't believe that I was now an orphan, I couldn't believe that I would never speak to my father again. I stayed in Sierra Leone for five days and returned back to the UK, My life was different, my heart was heavy but I had no choice but to look towards the future because I was about to become a mother. I found out that I was having a baby girl, I wanted a boy so badly because I couldn't deal with the idea of having a daughter which would mean I would have to address a lot of the trauma that I had hidden under my spiritual bed. She started kicking on the day I found out about my father's death and every time that I would start crying for my father she would become distressed and kick me for 30 minutes straight. People told me that it was a sign that she didn't want me to cry all the time and that she could sense my energy. I prayed everyday for strength and every day I reminded myself that although God permitted my Father to go, he also gave me my daughter as my comfort and reminder that I wasn't alone. On June 22nd 2013 at 08:24pm they lay her on my chest and she was the most amazing thing that I had ever seen. I was speechless as she cried and I looked at her in awe, My cousin Koya was by my side throughout my labor and she gave me strength in that labor room when I didn't have any. We both cried when she came out and straight away I saw my father in her and I thanked God because I knew that he was always going to be with me through the eyes of my baby girl.

I struggled as a new mother and learning the difficult things that they didn't tell me about but Koya was my strength, I would message her with all my questions and worries and each time she would make me feel in control and reminded me that I had nothing to be afraid off and told me all the time that I was a brilliant mother. I was at home caring for my daughter Gabriella and at a time when I should have been supported by my daughter's father I was still being emotionally abused, things became worse because he wanted to control my actions and thought that I would be a meal ticket for him to live off and that would never be the case. He was lazy and didn't want to work for anything and I was not the type of a woman that caters for a selfish and lazy man. He would call me to purposely start arguments with me and insult me; he would tell me that I was useless and that I had not achieved anything in my life and that I should be ashamed at my age I didn't even have a degree. It was clear to me that he wanted to break my confidence so that he could try to gain control of me but he was knocking on the wrong door because I gave him as good as I got. When my daughter was three months old I received information that my child's father was in a relationship with a girl in Sierra Leone, I was contacted by the girl's family and given all the information and I was told that my child's father's mother was aware of his other relationship. I was tired, fed up and ready to put an end to this situation, my father was gone and I had no one else to protect. I was ready to wear the single mother crown and I was prepared for whatever stories would come along with my decision to end the relationship. I prayed and I fasted and I asked God for the strength to move on with my life with my daughter and strength is what God gave me. I ended the relationship with him and right after I discovered that this man had a few other girlfriends scattered all around, all I could do was thank God that it was over and prepared myself for whatever was ahead of us. I believe that he sensed that I was happy about the break-up because I was over the arguing and all the abuse. The people I introduced to

him as my friends turned against me and were
sharing information about me to him and
making up lies. They wanted to see me in a
space of distress, at this time I had been given
my own two bedroom apartment for me and
Gabriella and I was working towards rebuilding
our lives and it started to occur to me that no
everyone was happy about the good things that
were happening in my life because that meant
they didn't have bad news to spread around. I
started distancing myself from a lot of people
and just focused on being a mother to my
daughter. I did my best to co-parent with my
child's father but he was salty that I broke up
with him so he used whatever he could to try
and punish me. He told me that no other man
would want me as second hand goods now
since I was raising a child alone, I came to see
his true identity and realised that he wasn't a
good or nice person and I thanked God
everyday that I was able to realise that he was
an abuser and I did not submit myself to
demands.

Raising my daughter alone was not the easiest
thing to do, I felt alone most of the time
regardless of how many friends were in my
life, I changed several jobs just to ensure that

my daughters care needs were met and I didn't want to place her in the care of anyone that I didn't trust just so that I could go to work, her life and safety was more important to me. There were many challenges that made me question whether or not I was able to truly care for her and the hardest challenge was when I had to leave my job and stay at home with her for almost two years because she was not settling at any nursery or child carer. She was a breastfed baby and I fed her until she was one years old so I assumed it was the attachment but even after I her pulled her off the breast she was still clingy, I didn't know what to do, I would cry and just wonder what I was doing wrong and everyone kept telling me that what I was actually doing was right. Aunty B told me one day that the best invest in this life isn't the houses or the cars or the degrees but rather our children, she said that Gabriella wasn't ready to be cared for by anyone else yet and I needed to wait until she was ready. I became self-employed and started a gift basket business, I started enjoying the time I spent at home with my daughter and watching her reach certain milestones it was priceless. As time passed my daughter's father became less present and I became less bothered

because I had one child to care for without any
support and I was not going to keep
encouraging a fully grown man to do what was
right by his daughter so in my mind and heart I
closed the chapter where I ever had hope that
he would step up and be the father that
Gabriella needed and I prayed that God would
choose a partner for me that would love and
accept my daughter as his own. I had gone
through so much in 2013 but I didn't lose hope
because losing my father almost sent me over
the age but the test that was given to me was
to overcome the loss in order for me to be able
to stand up tall and receive the testimony that
was my daughter Gabriella.

9 THE BITTER PILL OF LOVE (2018)

I had overcome so much with losing my father
in March 2013 and having Gabriella in June,
The day before I had Gabriella I received news
from America that my aunty Hilda had passed
way, the shock of the news is what sent me
into labor. Hilda was comforting me through my
father's death and we had even planned that
she would send my little cousin Hannah over to
the UK over the summer to spend time with me
and help me with the baby. I didn't understand
it and I was in shock, Aunty Hilda couldn't have
gone because I had just spoken to her recently,
this was another emotional blow that I found
hard to digest. A week after I had Gabriella my
brother Borboh passed away of a drug
overdose, I was numb and speechless, three

deaths in a few months who would I grieve
first. I tried my best to focus on being a mother
to Gabriella, I couldn't deal with the pain that
was pilling up around me, and it was too much
too soon. A few months later in October when
Gabriella was six months old Edward messaged
me that Aunty Binty had passed away and then
finally I lost it. What was happening in my life,
why was everyone that I loved dying, was it
me? Did something or someone in the world
not want me to be surrounded by my family? I
was in awe and in agony. I booked a ticket and
immediately flew out to the USA for Aunty
Binty's burial, seeing Edward and Elizabeth
made it harder because I was once in their
shoes and I knew exactly what they were
feeling and the worst part of that was knowing
the pain that they would have to deal with
every day after Auntie's burial.

Liz and Eddy loved their mother, they were the
joy and pride of Aunty Binty's heart and though
she always expressed to me about how many
mistakes she made in her young life and
advised me to not do the same all I saw was a
woman that had carried pain so effortlessly.
Aunty Binty lost her battle to cancer but I was
so proud that she fought for her life and I know

that she left a mark on the hearts of so many people and I know that the void she left in those hearts can never be filled. I slept in Auntie's room and everyone kept asking me if I wasn't afraid and I told them that I wasn't because of the bond I shared with her, I was okay after the burial and kept myself together until everyone came back to the house after the burial. I went to her room and I got changed and as I walked back down the stairs it finally hit me, Aunty Binty was gone, I would never be able to speak to her again and in that moment I broke down and started crying hysterically; Hannah and Lizzy comforted me and we spoke about the positive memories and all the great things Aunty did. The comfort was for a moment, that night I crawled into her bed and wore one of her cardigans and I cried myself to sleep, my adviser and comforter was gone, another gem had fallen from my glittery robe of blessings.

I returned back to the UK and continued with life, I kept Lizzy and Edward in my prayer intensely because I knew what they were up against emotionally. I did my best to check in with them and made sure that they were okay; although I was far away I was only a call away.

I became isolated because the three people that I confided in about my problems were gone, my dad was gone, Aunty Hilda was gone and now Aunty Binty was gone and I felt alone. Life came at me fast and some things and some people were uprooted and others were planted and I just went with the flow and believed that God was truly at work in my life. A relationship was not even on my radar, since the break up with my daughter's father I found it hard to have that genuine trust and interest in men. August 2015 I attended a friend's child's birthday party and there I met someone, we met as friends and we bonded very quickly over conversations about love and our interests. For me it was a friendship, though I did think he was cute but it was a friendship because I had heard so many things about him that I couldn't bring myself to like him. I didn't judge him on the basis of what everyone else said because what he showed me was that he was a respectful, calm and collected young man who seemed to be very open with me. I will call him YDB because that's what I would often change his name to on my phone whenever he would annoy me. From August till December 2015 me and YDB were talking every single day, I would wake up every day

with the sweetest good morning messages
from him and I must say as wrong as his game
was he played it very well because without
realising I fell in love. I made the first attempt
to end our communication because I hated how
I felt about him and I sensed that the situation
wasn't right but when I tried to cut him loose
he wouldn't let me and would draw me back in
emotionally. I really believed that he was
different because he moved different with me,
he told me all the right things and we had long
what's app voice and video calls and we
laughed and joked and everything was great
until it was time to take things to the next
level. There was always an issue when it was
that time, he would emotionally check out and
to me that was a sign that he didn't want to be
with me or he wasn't ready and I didn't have
time for games so I would try to cut him loose
but that never worked because he had game
with his words and I was dumb and in love. I
loved many things about YDB but what I loved
most was the love he had for my daughter, it
was an effortless and genuine, his face would
light up when he would speak to her on video
call and I loved that because I wanted to be
with a man that loved my daughter as much as
he loved me.

A year later we were in Sierra Leone and there I discovered that YDB that sold me the biggest lie of all, YDB had me in my feelings for more than a year thinking that there was something wrong with me, he kept stringing me along like a puppet. I found out that he had met a girl who he had started dating while he was still communicating with me and when I confronted him about the situation he lied and told me that it wasn't what I thought it was and that he would explain. He put me in a situation where this girl and her group of friends did everything possible to try and make my life miserable, they would mock me on social media and taunt me whenever they saw me in public and on some occasions I would go home and cry because yet again I had put myself in a situation with a man that refused to do right by me and now it was causing me shame and distress. YDB continued to deny his relationship with this girl until I saw them together with my own two eyes and even after that he refused to tell me that he was in a relationship with her. I called him on January 1st 2017 to have a heart to heart and pleaded with him to be honest and open with me about what was going on and finally he confessed and told me that he was in a relationship with her

and just like that he pulled the carpet from
under my feet and I fell hard. I returned to the
UK with a bitter sweet feeling in my heart, 80%
of me was broken and disappointed and
shocked at what he had done but the other 20%
was happy that finally this chapter was closed
and I could take steps towards healing and
moving on with my life. I couldn't help but feel
like a loser again, another broken relationship,
I started to feel as though I was the problem. I
started my own prayer group and focused my
time on rebuilding myself spiritually and letting
go of whatever hurt of pain I was feeling. A
few months passed and I started having a lot of
dreams about YDB and they were not good
dreams, I prayed and fasted and asked God to
help YDB with whatever it was that he was
going through. I had a dream that was so bad
that I couldn't ignore it, me and YDB use to
pray together and I would often have dreams
about him that were mirroring what exactly he
was going through. I contacted one of YDB's
friends and explained my dreams to him and
asked if YDB was okay and I was informed that
all was not well.

A day after I spoke to YDB's friend YDB
contacted me and told me that he heard about

my dreams and wanted us to talk, I gave him a time that would be suitable for us both and we scheduled a call. YDB called and asked about Gabriella and made some small talk before asking me about the dreams I had. I explained everything to him and he informed me that my dreams are speaking of what he is presently going through. I gave him spiritual advice and prayed with him and encouraged him to pray daily. He confided in me about a lot of things and also made some confessions about things he has previously lied to me about and that gave me cause for concern which made me suggest that we start reading the bible and praying together. YDB was happy and thanked me and we scheduled a time that we would read the bible and pray together every day. After the phone call I received a text from him thanking me for everything and apologising to me for the way he had treated me and told me that I had a very forgiving heart.

We started our prayers in March 2017 and we prayed and fasted until November 2017 and during this time YDB was going through a lot emotionally and spiritually, I became his vessel, I poured everything out of myself and into him. Feelings from the past started to creep in, we were talking every single day for over eight months so it was expected. We argued and made up, screamed at each other and made up, blocked and unblocked; it was a rollercoaster of emotions and it seemed that there were forces fighting against our prayers. Everyone around me was concerned, no one supported me speaking to him or helping him in any kind of way but I was adamant that I needed too. My friends pleaded with me to not open my heart to him again but it was too late, I was back in love and I thought that I saw change in him. No matter how many times we argued and tried to walk away from each other something always seemed to draw us back together. YDB and the girl he was dating had broken up, he messaged me at 5am in the morning telling me that she was caught cheating with someone that YDB knew and also with one of her friend's boyfriends and he was sent the proof. I didn't want to be a part of his drama or even in this love triangle that didn't even need to exist but I had a soft spot for him and I couldn't turn my back on him. YDB was having many spiritual attacks and through all of that we continued to pray, he was given certain warnings by people close to him and by spiritual advisers about the girl that he was

dating but YDB ignored. In February 2018 I
went to Sierra Leone to work on one of my
business projects that I had brought YDB into, I
was aware that even after YDB found out about
the girl's infidelities he continued to sleep with
her but denied to everyone that they were no
longer together. When I arrived in town I saw
the full picture of what was really happening
and realised that YDB had me caught in his
web of lies again. On Valentine's Day we went
to YDB's parent's house and he told me he
wanted me to meet his parents, as I waited in
the hallway I was given his phone by his cousin
to make a professional phone call for him; but
something told me that this was my time to
seek all the answers he wasn't giving me for
the past few years. I went into the toilet and
locked myself in and started going through his
phone, I felt as though a knife was being pulled
through my heart with what I discovered, I was
devastated. YDB had girlfriends, not just the
girl we had the issue with but another girl that
I had suspected that he had relations with but
he denied that he didn't. My heart was racing
as I came across text messages and call logs
that painted a clear picture to me of how
manipulating and condescending this man had
been. I sat down in that toilet and I cried

because I couldn't understand how someone could be so wicked, how he could continue to lie to me and break my spirit continuously when all I ever did was pour love into him while he took it away from me. I confronted him about what I had seen when we left his parents house and he made excuses but none of them worked for me so in the end he just confessed everything. I cried a lot that day, I was crying because I knew this was the end of the road for me and YDB because I started to clearly see that he had taken me for granted for way too long and this was no longer a matter of patience because I had given him years to do right by me and he chose not to.

I am ashamed to confess that even with all that he had done I couldn't let him go emotionally because I was so deeply in love, I could see clearly that he was tiring me apart and breaking my heart but I was ready to have any piece of him that he gave me as long as I had him in some way. It wasn't about not knowing my self-worth or understanding that deserved way more than I was getting; it was about me trying to avoid the pain yet again. I wasn't prepared to have to deal with the disappointment, the shame and the opinions of

people if this didn't work. I had pushed other
men away and I was loyal to a man that was
never loyal to me, I acted as if we were in a
relationship rather than a situationship. I gave
YDB the best of me; I gave him husband
privileges when he wasn't even a boyfriend.
We lived happily for exactly a week until he
finally threw the bomb that broke down the
walls of my heart. Yet again YDB betrayed me
but this time it was worse because he promised
me that he had changed, I saw the change, and
I saw him trying. He had cut ties with the other
girls and he was focused on me. We got into a
argument when I caught him in traffic with the
same girl he had told me if ended things with, I
was enraged and so angry because now it felt
like he was trying to openly disgrace me and I
didn't understand what I had done to deserve
this. I called him and asked him to come and
take his things from my house and that I was
finally done with him, he probably thought I
was just speaking out of anger and that I would
calm down and he would be able to pull the
wool over my eyes again. My rage was
uncontrollable, I was so broken and ashamed, I
started drinking vodka because the pain in my
heart was physical and nothing made me feel
better. My friends pleaded with me to calm

down but I was screaming and crying in the house and cursing him and the entire time he was on the other side of the phone laughing at me and acted like my pain as a joke, he saw me as a laughing stock; was this the same man that I spent years praying for? The same man that told me that he could see me as his wife? Was I dreaming?.

The Vodka worked and I went from zero to 7000 in a few hours, we argued for a few hours over the phone and he later came to my house with the police to collect his things. He was so bold and confident as If I was his enemy, he told the police that he feared for his safety which is why he came with them to the house. I had burnt some of his clothes earlier in the day but was that an excuse to come to my home with the police; Lisa Left eye Lopez burnt down an entire house in the name of love. YDB and his cousin went into the bedroom to go and take his remaining clothes and shoes and he was acting all cocky and confident as if he didn't already know that I was ready throw him in the lion's den I was that angry. He started making sly comments to me so I picked up one of his shoes and aimed to throw it at his head but it missed him because he started running to

the front of the house where the police was.
The police asked YDB's cousin to hold me in
one of the rooms while YDB left the house
because at this point we had started arguing, I
was locked in a room trying to get away from
his cousin, I struggled and I screamed for him
to let me go and he wouldn't as he begged me
" FA please please calm down, I know you're
hurting and I know you're in pain but please
don't do this please ", his plea meant nothing to
me, I was drunk and angry and I was tired of
being the bigger person. I had decided that this
would be the last time he would do this to me, I
needed to make sure that it was the last time;
something needed to happen that would finally
separate us and with that thought I managed to
get away from YDB's cousin and I ran and
opened the room door, I picked up a speaker
cable with an mental top on my way out the
house and I ran so fast, out the house and into
the street and there was YDB's car driving
away. He was not going to leave me broken
again, he was not going to leave me in sorrow
again, I wanted him to remember me so I ran
and caught up with the car and with the metal
cable in my hand I smashed the back of his car
window. Everyone in the street screamed and
his car stopped, I was breathing with intensity

and the deed was done so I ran back into the house and locked myself in my bedroom and called my Uncle Abu and told him what I had done and told him that I was about to be arrested. I started preparing myself as the police officers came back into the compound and asked me to come out. They were screaming and shouting and telling me that I had no respect for them as authorities of the law, what law I thought; they came to my house because YDB had paid them too, so the real disrespect was the fact that they left their duty posts at 9pm at night to bottle feed an overgrown womaniser while they ignored the real crime of young girls being raped in the same city daily.

They arrested me, YDB, his cousin and the three police officers all went into the car and they drove me to the station where they were posted. My Uncle sent my brother and a family friend to come and represent me at the station and some of my friends and my cousin Tehsie were also there to support me. YDB was on fire, he was acting as though I had killed someone, did this man forget that we were sharing a bed just a few days before? Were we not waking up next to each other? Was I not running your bath water and cooking you breakfast? Didn't I put the toothpaste on your tooth brush every morning before you woke up?. I sat in silence as I watched his ego grow, he said that I wasn't remorseful and needed to be taught a lesson. My uncle's friend pleaded with the police and YDB for the case to be settled outside the station but YDB didn't agree, so after our statements were taken I was officially arrested and read my rights and I was placed in a cell. I gave Tehsie my phone and jewellery as I sat down in that dark cell that smelt like a dirty toilet and I started praying. I asked God to forgive me for allowing my anger to get the best of me and kept praying for peace and asked him grant me the strength to forgive YDB for what he was doing to me and what he would later do. My Asthma started playing up and I started having panic attacks, my friend Bjorn heard the news and he came to the police station at 1am in the morning and demanded that I was taken out of that cell, he told the officers that it was injustice and YDB offended me first and had been doing so for a while. Bjorn spoke to the officers and asked to keep me in a place with air and light because of my health condition, everyone left and went home and there I was at a police station under arrest because of love, what was I thinking? I started regretting ever meeting YDB because this was a lot of pain to carry. I Cried the entire night, the officers on duty started pleading with me to stop crying and started to comfort and told me that sometimes we end up paying a big price for love. The next morning my uncle Francis, Bjorn, my friends and Tehsie all came to the station, YDB came strolling through the station like a man on a mission, I looked at him and for a second I just felt sorry for him because I was sure that whoever was behind this encouraging him to do what he was doing to me didn't truly understand our history and I knew that no matter how painful it felt I knew it would all pass and one day I would be able to look back at this situation and praise God.

YDB was adamant that I should pay him for the broken glass which was fair enough if that is how he felt. My Uncle and other people around us begged him to close the case and settle it between ourselves but YDB refused and was enraged as he made a sense in front of my Uncle about being paid the money that was owed to him for his car window. I was so ashamed, I sat down in front of the police officer, my Uncle and YDB as we tried to come to an agreement and when I looked over I saw tears flowing from my Uncles eyes and in that moment I realised that my actions this time had affected the people that I loved and that was the highest level of shame for me. YDB made everything so difficult, he acted as though I was nothing to him and everything that people had said about him that I had ignored started to surface. I was charged £250 for his window and I paid up, but before I paid I cried a lot; my friend Diaka was livid, she had warned me to be careful with YDB because she was sure he would disappointment me again. But like a real friend she stood by me throughout the process, when I was in bed crying she would come by my side and comfort me and tell me that I was better off without him; he got me arrested she was at the station with me, I was betrayed by the people I least expected but my friend Diaka stood with me like a real sister. The rest of my holiday was full of sorrow, nothing was fun anymore, and I smiled when I needed too but I was walking with a bleeding heart that ached every time I thought about what YDB had done to me. He went back to the girl he said was his ex and they did everything possible to make sure that I knew, the news was all around town and people actually called to sympathise with me and encouraged me to move on with my life and told me that YDB was never good enough for me because he liked women of a lower class and that was something I never really understood.

I stood at Lungi airport with Gabriella as we waited in line to board the plane back to the UK, I couldn't control my tears so I started crying and crying and crying and Gabriella just wrapped her tiny arms around my legs as she tried to comfort me. I didn't want my daughter to see me in that state and I tried everything to not cry but I couldn't control my emotions. There was a Liberian man stood behind me and he tapped me on the shoulder and said "My dear I've seen you crying for a while now, you are way too beautiful to be crying so much what's wrong ", I couldn't speak because I was trying to stop myself from crying more so I just said I was okay and turned away as I wiped away my tears. I cried all the way to the UK on a ten hour transit journey. Diaka called me as soon as I landed and we spoke on the ride home from the airport and she advised me to focus on Gabriella and leave YDB in the past and told me that as always I should allow God to be my defender, no truer words were spoken and I was ready to let go. I spent the first week in bed crying, for the first time in my life I couldn't control my tears, I lost my appetite and withdrew from a lot people because the rumors of what had happened had spread around the Sierra Leonean community and I was ashamed. YDB was so wicked, he never for one second thought about what I was going through but instead he was on social media everyday declaring his love for his girlfriend, I left the company where we both worked because I couldn't take the disrespect anymore, I brought him into that company at a time when he needed hope, when he was broken and he used that same platform to try and break me and disrespect me by using his girlfriend to advertise the business. I found out two months later that YDB was expecting a baby with his girlfriend, he was parading everything on social media for the world to see and people started to gossip about me and make up their own versions of what they believed the truth was, they labeled me as the side chick that was forcing herself on him and he never wanted to be with me is what they said. It was the shame that drove me into depression, I went from a size 12 to a size 8;

my peace was gone, I prayed and fasted so much because that was the only thing that kept me sane, I was grieving for the loss of a relationship that never existed and while I was dealing with my pain I had to deal with the reality that he never cared for me, he used me as his buffer; I would pick him up and dust him off and he would go right back to those that broke him down and I was always there to pick up the pieces. 2018 was just an unbearable year for me, I was fighting battles that the world didn't know about and a point came when I wanted to take my life because it felt like everything and everyone was against me. The people I thought were my friends turned out to me my enemies, they were the ones talking about me behind my back and helping to spread the lies. Even people in my own family betrayed me, I was belittled and disrespected on levels that I thought people would never reach and these were people I had been good too, people that had eaten from the goodness of my hands.

I celebrated my 31st birthday and on that day I made a promise to God that never again would any man treat me less than I deserved. I vowed to never allow any man to feed me with their lies and keep me locked up in their emotional cage of abuse. Throughout 2018 I realised that every relationship I had been in was emotionally abusive, the breakdown of the situation with YDB caused me to have to examine myself and see where I was going wrong, what was I doing that permitted these men to treat me this way. Koya always tells me that we attract the reflection of ourselves, so if I was attracting men that seemed to have it all together but where actually broken men then that meant that I was broken. Instead of dealing with my own trauma I tried to fix theirs because it is much easier to blow the dirty out of someone else's eyes instead of looking into your own. I was able to truly understand that I had to deal with the trauma in my past, I have to pull it out, cry it out and let go of it. I needed to stop allowing people to manipulate me into being in situations with them longer than I needed to me, realised that I had been emotionally abused by family, friends and lovers all my life and I just saw that as something that was a part of life and normal when the reality was that I had the power to make those changes. I prayed so much and I kept the focus on me, I forgave YDB for everything he had done to me because the bitterness I felt towards him was too big and I couldn't carry that. I allowed myself to be angry and to hate him for a while but in the end I just let it go and told God that I never meant YDB any harm and I prayed that God would be my comforter and defender against all the lies that the enemies had built against me. In my time of sorrow I had God, I had my bible and God sent the most unlikely people to be my comfort during that time. He sent those that cried with me and wiped away my tears without judgment or expectation. I fought the battle against depression, I fought the battle against insanity, I fought the battle against suicide and I fought those demons in a dark tunnel but as always Jesus held a light before me as I walked past the mess of my life. YDB made me question my self-worth and confidence because so many times he would build my hope up and stab me in the heart as soon as it was time for him to deliver what he promised. As 2018 came to an end I was fighting against everything and everyone that wanted this situation to be what would break me and God gave me " Isaiah 61:7 " Instead of shame you will receive double portion, and instead of disgrace you will rejoice in your inheritance, you will inherit a double portion in

your land and everlasting joy will be yours ".
That scripture is what pulled me out of the
darkness, I would pray and cry over it as I
waited for God to give me a reason to smile
again, I really thought that it was the end for
me and I had fought so many battles but I
thought this one would break me but it didn't,
Instead I learnt the greatest lesson of my life,
you cannot control the actions of others but
you have power over how you react to them. I
had experienced all types of pain and trauma in
my life and I overcame them but for the first
time in my life I had to taste, chew and swallow
the bitter pill of love.

10 NOT EASILY BROKEN

I have made so many mistakes that I carried as weight, I have learnt to let go of the past and focus on the things in front of me. Gabriella has truly been my strength, I believe that God gave her to me at the right time, a time when I needed hope and when I was lacking faith because of the things that were happening around me. I told myself that I needed to keep pushing and moving forward because if I focused on the things that were happening to me I would break down. I have been good to people and most times they are not always good to me in return, I always tell God that I was born in the wrong generation because I find it so difficult to fit in with the state of this world.

I have met people who just hate me for no reason and people who go out of their way to try and tarnish my character, I always wonder what it is about me that causes irritation to them, some of them have some of the things I am still waiting for God to give me to me yet they see me as a threat. I started telling myself that I may be better off without friends and I started drawing closer to family and that turned out to be the worst battle I faced. I've had to deal with sibling rivalry or siblings that are always finding a way to place blame on me or tarnish my character so that other people won't like me but in all of those moments I remained true to myself and who I was and did not allow anyone to change the goodness in my heart.

I didn't have the easiest start in life, my battles started in my mother's womb and I was born innocent to the forces of darkness that seemed to be after me life. I have taken every battle with a pinch of salt and kept moving forward without complaining about my scares or opened wounds. I have been abused sexually, physically and emotionally but through all of that my beacon of hope came from God, I found God when I was 17 years old while dealing with my mother's death, I lost him a few times while I was busy making my mistakes and running away from him out of shame but every time I cried he was there to wipe away my tears. People always ask why my faith is so rooted when they want to challenge me on the basis of the religion I follow. How do I explain to anyone about something that they cannot see or feel, how can I explain the supernatural things that God shows me that manifest physically but they call me crazy. I can't explain who God is and show anyone a physical picture but I can testify that throughout the sorrowful moments of my life he was there, when I did the things that I now regret he was there; never judging or withholding my blessings but always keeping his arms open for me. They can never understand my praise because they haven't witnessed my pain, they haven't seen me in a state of brokenness when I drank bottles and bottles of alcohol to numb the pain in my heart, they haven't witnessed the countless times when I was a teenager and I swallowed pills to try and take my own life because I couldn't deal with the memories of my abusers. Where were they when the devil held my hand as I threw my first baby away, where were they when I tried so hard to wash the blood from my hands because I couldn't deal the loss of my child. When I was on my knees screaming for my baby, when I was bleeding as they ripped him out of me, where were they when I carried that guilt with me for so long as I didn't think I ever deserved to have a child. It was him, my God, my redeemer; the mighty one of Jacob that called me back home. It was my church that wiped away those tears and told me that I needed to forgive myself and let go of that weight, the hardest realisation was that the people that are now exposed as my enemies were the same people who encouraged me and pushed me to make those choices. I cannot place the blame on them but I hold them accountable for preying on me during my time of weakness. They wanted to bury me so badly, so they started digging the biggest pit and they kicked me down and they buried me under and covered me with soil without a second thought because they wanted my life. Their disgrace came when they realised that I didn't die, the soil didn't kill me because my father in heaven poured and poured and continued to pour rain, and as the rain fell on me under that soil I was crying, fighting for air; I didn't have enough air but I was breathing and then just as they thought I had stopped moving; up came what they buried. I wasn't a dead vessel, I wasn't an empty element, I am a seed, planted by the trees of righteousness and by the grace of my God.

I know that there are forces that want me dead,

they do not want to see me shine, so they plot and they plan but I know that my redeemer lives and no matter what the world throws at me I will overcome it, raise above it because I am a beloved daughter of Zion so I always rises up. When I look back at my life today I look back with happiness and pride because I know that God permitted those things to happen in my life because he knew that I was a vessel that he can use to turn those tests into testimonies and I would not be afraid to share my painful and shameful stories with the rest of the world if it would be a comfort for someone. If it will save a soul and bring someone out of the darkness then all the pain was worth it as long as the glory is always given to God, I am thankful for all the experiences bitter and sweet that I was able to taste and digest and I am now able to withstand some of the storms that would have knocked me down before. I am thankful to the men who I once shared love with, Abdul, Didi and YDB, even though it may have ended bitterly I am so sure body, soul, mind and spirit that in those moments of happiness it meant more than I can account for today I only take away the positive memories and I leave the bitterness in the hands of devil. I have been molded by all my experiences and today I stand tall as a woman who is sure of who she is and what she wants out of the universe, I am not ashamed of my experiences good or bad and I proudly showcase my scares as my badges from all the battles that I am overcome. I was told so many negative things about myself that I could have believed but instead I chose to accept that I am an extraordinary woman who is unique and that uniqueness is what the world hates and I am proud to say that I am ready for whatever they want to throw my way because my life has been the best teacher to me. I am brave, I am sure, I am confident and forever I stand against all the lies and believe the one truth to be that........ I AM NOT EASILY BROKEN.

ABOUT THE AUTHOR

FA Bockari (Fatmata Bockari) is a writer, mother and philanthropist who works to motivate young girls and single mothers, She is also the owner of Project_1625 a community organization that works to bring inclusion, empowerment and equality for young people locally and internationally.

43635423R00143

Printed in Poland
by Amazon Fulfillment
Poland Sp. z o.o., Wrocław